Learning Facebook Application Development

A step-by-step tutorial for creating custom Facebook applications using the Facebook platform and PHP

Hasin Hayder

Dr. Mark Alexander Bain

BIRMINGHAM - MUMBAI

Learning Facebook Application Development

First published: May 2008

Production Reference: 1200508

Published by Packt Publishing Ltd.
32 Lincoln Road
Olton
Birmingham, B27 6PA, UK.

ISBN 978-1-847193-69-8

www.packtpub.com

Cover Image by Nilesh Mohite (nilpreet2000@yahoo.co.in)

Credits

Authors

Hasin Hayder

Dr. Mark Alexander Bain

Reviewers

Junal Rahman

Md. Nur Hossain

Senior Acquisition Editor

David Barnes

Development Editor

Nikhil Bangera

Technical Editor

Ajay Shanker

Editorial Team Leader

Mithil Kulkarni

Project Manager

Abhijeet Deobhakta

Indexer

Hamangini Bari

Proofreader

Camille Guy

Production Coordinator

Aparna Bhagat

Cover Work

Aparna Bhagat

About the Authors

Hasin Hayder, graduated in Civil Engineering from the Rajshahi University of Engineering and Technology (RUET) in Bangladesh. He is a Zend-certified Engineer and expert in developing localized applications. He is currently working as a Technical Director in Trippert Labs and managing the local branch in Bangladesh. Beside his full time job, Hasin writes his blog at http://hasin.wordpress.com, writes article in different websites and maintains his open-source framework Orchid at http://orchid.phpxperts.net. Hasin lives in Bangladesh with his wife Ayesha and his son, Afif.

Thanks goes to my colleagues at TrippertLabs and phpExperts, for supporting me during this time. Thanks to Abhijeet, Nikhil, and David for their patience while I was late. And definitely, thanks to my family members, especially Ayesha and Afif for their support.

Dr. Mark Alexander Bain first started customizing CRM systems back in the mid '90s when he was team leader for Vodafone's Cascade project—the team took the 'out-of-the-box' Clarify CRM and turned it into a radio base station planning application, complete with a workflow engine for passing jobs between the different departments involved in the planning, building, and implementation of a radio network. Since then, he's lectured at the University of Central Lancashire. Currently Mark writes articles on all things Linux and Open Source for Linux Format, Newsforge.com and Linux Journal. SugarCRM customization, therefore, seems the obvious choice for this, his second book, since it combines Mark's knowledge of working with commercial CRMs and the Open Source philosophy. Mark works from his home on the edge of the Lake District in the UK, where he lives with his wife, two dogs and two cats, and gets the odd visit from his sons—Michael and Simon.

About the Reviewers

Junal Rahman is a Computer Science graduate from Independent University of Bangladesh. His areas of expertise include programming with .Net and PHP framework. He has worked for several software companies as a web application developer. During his undergraduate studies, Junal completed his internship program at Alliance Creation where he worked on several projects including a garments inventory system for Opti Garments. Following his graduation, he became a full-time employee at Alliance Creation and continued working with the PHP framework. Later, he moved on to work for Systech Digital where he became a PHP team leader, managing and supervising projects for Systech Digital clients. As an aside, during his time at Alliance Creation and Systech Digital, Junal worked for a freelancing company called Allomatch as a freelance developer, where he gained experience in Smarty, a unique programming language. Finally, he joined Trippert Labs, where he now works as a Development Engineer. At Trippert, Junal works collaboratively to create Facebook applications. Apart from keeping up with the ever changing field of information technology, he spends much of his private life pursing his interests in screenplay and script writing. In the future, Junal hopes to create films and short dramas, and eventually establish his very own software company.

I would like to thank Hasin Hayder, my mentor, for writing this amazing book and dedicate my effort to my maternal uncle Shafiqul Karim for his eternal inspiration and continual encouragement.

Md. Nur Hossain is a B.Sc graduate from Shahjalal University of Science & Technology specializing in Computer Science & Engineering. For the past four years, he has been working in the field of web development and performance tuning. His area of interest is design pattern and efficiency of large DB schema. He is currently working as a senior developer at Trippert Labs.

I am thankful to my parents who are always encouraging. Thank you Abhijeet, for managing the resources and communications so smoothly. And thanks Hasin, and all my colleagues for sharing your tremendous knowledge with me.

To you, the mastermind behind each and every Facebook application.

Table of Contents

Preface

Using Facebook applications, developers can add custom features to one of the most popular websites in the world. Facebook is the biggest social network among college students, and is gaining ground among professionals too. Facebook applications enable you to add new ways for users to interact with each other using Facebook.

Facebook applications are written in a server-side language, and hosted on the application developer's own server. They interface with Facebook, so that they appear to users to be part of Facebook itself.

This book shows PHP developers how to quickly get started building powerful Facebook applications, how to work with data stored in Facebook, including photos, and how to handle multimedia and other custom data within Facebook applications.

The book covers how to send notifications and invitations from within an application, update a user's profile, create application control panels for users, and much more.

What This Book Covers

Chapter 1 takes a look at the elements used by your application to interface with Facebook — the Facebook API, FBML, and FQL — that is the Facebook Platform.

Chapter 2 will cover how to extract the Facebook information to be displayed by your application, store information in the Facebook cache so that it can be displayed on your users' Profile pages, and store your own custom data.

Chapter 3 will cover how to manipulate data stored in a database, update your users' profiles automatically, track the users who are using your application, and use the Facebook Dashboard.

Chapter 4 will help you understand Facebook tags to display information in a hassle free and easier way. You will also get an introduction to Facebook Query Language (FQL), and understand why it is sometimes more effective to use FQL rather than the Facebook REST API.

Chapter 5 will see the scripting ability in Facebook, using a subset of standard JavaScript functions developed by Facebook, which is called FBJS.

Chapter 6 will go into the details of managing feeds (both news feed and mini feed) using Facebook REST APIs.

Chapter 7 will focus on creating a successful invitation system, creating a successful notification system, using notifications efficiently, and sending emails.

Chapter 8 will show you how to do the following: creating a photo importer from Facebook, creating a slide show application, and letting viewers upload photos to your album.

Chapter 9 will cover the usage of various tags in Facebook and create an interesting project using them.

Conventions

In this book, you will find a number of styles of text that distinguish between different kinds of information. Here are some examples of these styles, and an explanation of their meaning.

There are three styles for code. Code words in text are shown as follows: "We can include other contexts through the use of the `include` directive."

A block of code will be set as follows:

```
canpost="true"
candelete="false"
canmark="true"
cancreatetopic="true"
```

When we wish to draw your attention to a particular part of a code block, the relevant lines or items will be made bold:

```
index.php
<?
include_once("prepend.php"); //the Lib and key container
?>
```

New **terms** and **important words** are introduced in a bold-type font. Words that you see on the screen, in menus or dialog boxes for example, appear in our text like this: "clicking the **Next** button moves you to the next screen".

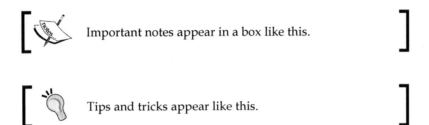

Important notes appear in a box like this.

Tips and tricks appear like this.

Reader Feedback

Feedback from our readers is always welcome. Let us know what you think about this book, what you liked or may have disliked. Reader feedback is important for us to develop titles that you really get the most out of.

To send us general feedback, simply drop an email to feedback@packtpub.com, making sure to mention the book title in the subject of your message.

If there is a book that you need and would like to see us publish, please send us a note in the **SUGGEST A TITLE** form on www.packtpub.com or email suggest@packtpub.com.

If there is a topic that you have expertise in and you are interested in either writing or contributing to a book, see our author guide on www.packtpub.com/authors.

Customer Support

Now that you are the proud owner of a Packt book, we have a number of things to help you to get the most from your purchase.

Downloading the Example Code for the Book

Visit http://www.packtpub.com/files/code/3698_Code.zip to directly downlad the example code.

The downloadable files contain instructions on how to use them.

Errata

Although we have taken every care to ensure the accuracy of our contents, mistakes do happen. If you find a mistake in one of our books—maybe a mistake in text or code—we would be grateful if you would report this to us. By doing this you can save other readers from frustration, and help to improve subsequent versions of this book. If you find any errata, report them by visiting http://www.packtpub.com/support, selecting your book, clicking on the **Submit Errata** link, and entering the details of your errata. Once your errata are verified, your submission will be accepted and the errata are added to the list of existing errata. The existing errata can be viewed by selecting your title from http://www.packtpub.com/support.

Questions

You can contact us at questions@packtpub.com if you are having a problem with some aspect of the book, and we will do our best to address it.

1
Getting to Grips with the Facebook Platform

If you've read even this far, then it's safe for me to assume that you're already well acquainted with Facebook, and (given the name of this book) it's also fairly safe to assume that you don't want an in-depth discussion on how to use Facebook—you just want to get on with building a Facebook application. So, that's exactly what we're going to do—we're going to build *Pygoscelis P. Ellsworthy's Suspect Tracker* as an example:

However, before we jump into building a Facebook application, we need to spend some time looking at the Facebook platform, and by the end of this chapter you will:

- Understand what the Facebook Platform is, and how it relates to your application

- Know about the elements that make up the Facebook Platform, and how to test them without having to create an application

- Know how to set up the Facebook Platform, ready for your new application

The Purpose of the Facebook Platform

As you develop your Facebook applications, you'll find that the Facebook Platform is essential—in fact you won't really be able to do anything without it. So what does it do? Well, before answering that, let's look at a typical web-based application.

The Standard Web Application Model

If you've ever designed and built a web application before, then you'd have done it in a fairly standard way. Your application and any associated data would have been placed on a web server, and then your application users will access it from their web browsers via the Internet:

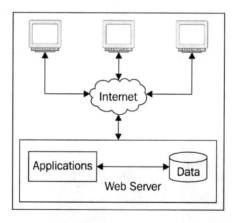

The Facebook model is slightly different.

The Facebook Web Application Model

As far as your application users are concerned, they will just access Facebook.com and your application, by using a web browser and the Internet. But, that's not where the application lives—*it's actually on your own server:*

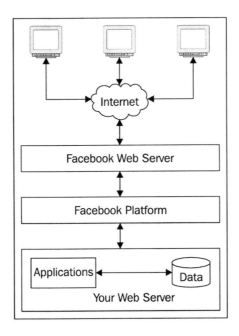

Once you've looked at the Facebook web application model and realized that your application actually resides on your own server, it becomes obvious what the purpose of the Facebook Platform is—to provide an interface between your application and itself.

There is an important matter to be considered here. If the application actually resides on your server, and your application becomes very successful (according to Facebook there are currently 25 million active users), then will your server be able to able to cope with that number of hits?

Don't be *too* alarmed. This doesn't mean that your server will be accessed every time someone looks at his or her profile. Facebook employs a cache to stop that happening:

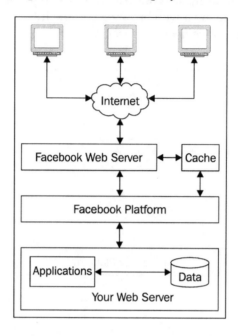

Of course, at this stage, you're probably more concerned with just getting the application working—so let's continue looking at the Platform, but just bear that point in mind.

The Facebook Platform Elements

There are three elements to the Facebook Platform:

- The Facebook API (Application Programming Interface)
- FBML—Facebook Markup Language
- FQL—Facebook Query Language

We'll now spend some time with each of these elements, and you'll see how you can use them individually, and in conjunction to make powerful yet simple applications. The great thing is that if you haven't got your web server set up yet, don't worry, because Facebook supplies you with all of the tools that you would need in order to do a test run with each of the elements.

The Facebook API

If you've already done some programming, then you'll probably know what an API (or Application Programming Interface) is. *It's a set of software libraries that enable you to work with an application (in this case, Facebook) without knowing anything about its internal workings.* All you have to do is obtain the libraries, and start making use of them in your own application.

Now, before you start downloading files, you can actually learn more about their functionality by making use of the Facebook API Test Console.

The Facebook API Test Console

If you want to make use of the Facebook Test Console, you'll first need to access the Facebook developers' section—you'll find a link to this at the bottom of every Facebook page:

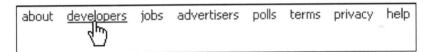

Alternatively, you can use the URL http://developers.facebook.com to go there directly in your browser. When you get to this page, you'll find a link to the **Tools** page:

Tools
Prototype your Facebook Platform application in real-time with easy-to-use test consoles.

Or, again, you can go directly to `http://developers.facebook.com/tools.php`, where you'll find the API Test Console:

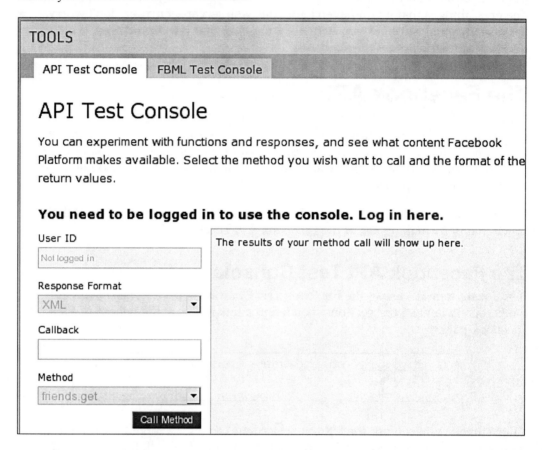

You'll find that the API Test Console has a number of fields:

- **User ID**—A read-only field which (when you're logged on to Facebook) unsurprisingly displays your user ID number.

- **Response Format**—With this, you can select the type of response that you want, and this can be:

    ◦ XML

    ◦ JSON

    ◦ Facebook PHP Client

- **Callback**—If you are using XML or JSON, then you can encapsulate the response in a function.

- **Method**—The actual Facebook method that you want to test.

Once you've logged in, you'll see that your User ID is displayed, and that all the drop-downs are enabled:

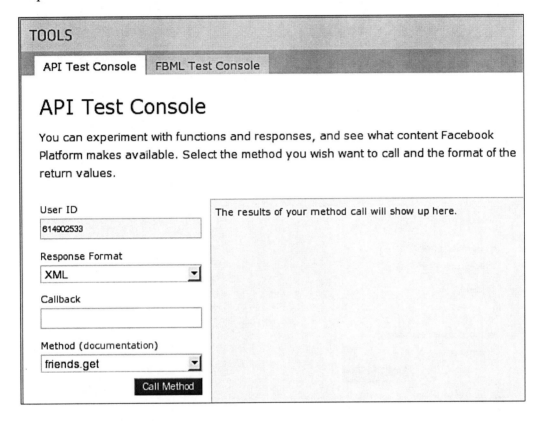

You will also notice that a new link, **documentation**, appears on the screen, which is very useful. All you have to do is to select a method from the drop-down list, and then click on **documentation**. Once you've done that you'll see:

- A description of the method
- The parameters used by the method
- An example return XML
- A description of the expected response.
- The FQL equivalent (we will discuss this later in the chapter.)
- Error codes

For now, let's just change the **Response Format** to **Facebook PHP Client,** and then click on **Call Method** to see what happens:

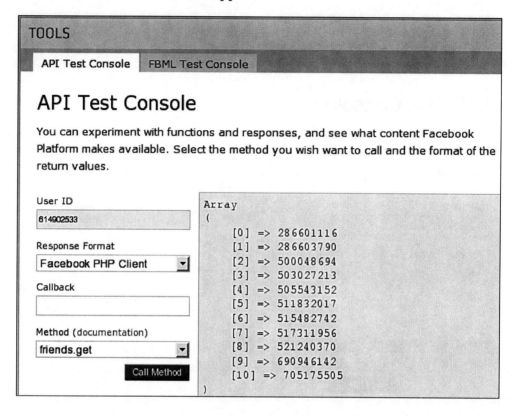

In this case, you can see that the method returns an array of user ids — each one being the ID of one of the friends of the currently logged in user (that is your list of friends because you're the person logged in). You could, of course, go on to use this array in PHP as part of your application, but don't worry about that at the moment. We'll see how to use the methods in a real application, in Chapter 2. For the time being, we'll just concentrate on working with our prototyping in the test console.

However, before we move on, it's worth noting that you can obtain an array of friends only for the currently logged in user. You can't obtain the list of friends for any other user. So, for example, you would not be able to use friends.get on id 286601116 or 705175505. In fact, you wouldn't be able to use friends.get for 614902533 (as shown in the example) because that's my ID and not yours.

On the other hand, having obtained a list of valid IDs we can now do something more interesting with them. For example, we can use the users.getinfo method to obtain the first name and birthday for particular users:

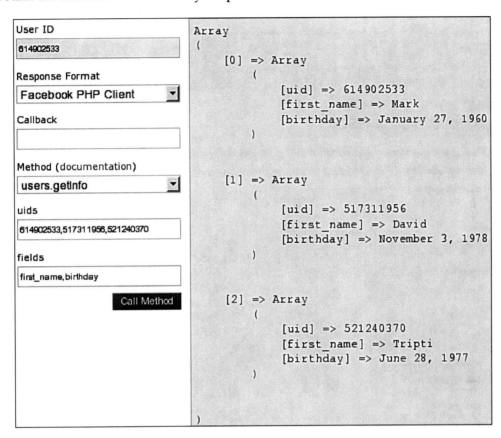

As you can see, a multidimensional array is returned to your PHP code (if you were actually using this in an application).Therefore, for example, if you were to load the array into a variable $birthdays, then $birthdays[0][birthday] would contain January 27, 1960.

Of course, in the above example, the most important piece of information is the first birthday in the array—record that in your diary for future reference. And, if you're thinking that I'm old enough to be your father, well, in some cases this is actually true:

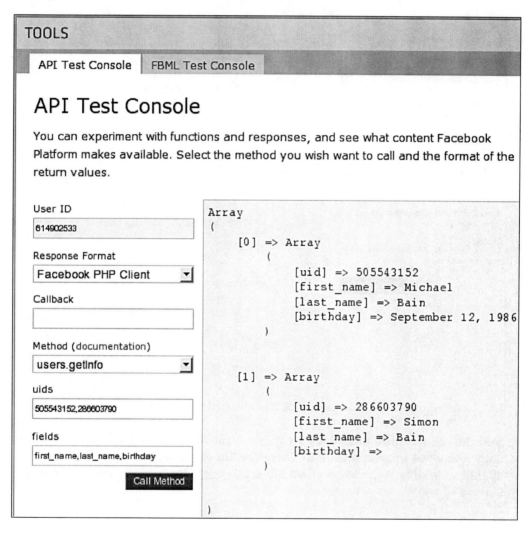

Now that you've come to grips with the API Test console, we can turn our attention to FBML and the FBML Test Console.

FBML

FBML, as mentioned previously, is the Facebook Markup Language. If you've used HTML in web pages, then you'll have no problem with FBML. Even if you've not used HTML ever, you'll still have no problems with FBML. It can be used to format your information just like HTML, but it also does a lot more than just formatting as we'll soon see, by looking at the FBML Test Console.

The FBML Test Console

We've already seen that we can learn how to use the Facebook API methods in the API Test Console, and we can do the same with FBML in the FBML Test Console. Just go to the **Tools** page as you did for the API Test Console, but this time click on the **FBML Test Console** tab:

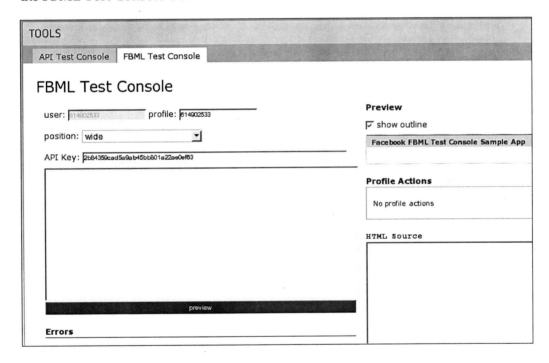

In this console, we're mainly interested in two areas:

- The code entry box—this is the large box on the left-hand-side of the console
- The preview area on the top-right of the console

Next, we need some code to test:

```
<table cellpadding=0 cellspacing=0><tr><td>
 <table cellpadding=0 cellspacing=0>
 <tr><td>
  <fb:profile-pic uid=614902533></fb:profile-pic>
 </td></tr>
 <tr><td>
  <fb:name useyou=false uid=614902533 firstnameonly=true></fb:name>
 </td></tr></table>
</td><td>
 <table cellpadding=0 cellspacing=0><tr><td>
  <fb:profile-pic uid=286603790></fb:profile-pic>
 </td></tr>
 <tr><td>
  <fb:name useyou=false uid=286603790 firstnameonly=true></fb:name>
 </td></tr></table>
</td><td>
 <table cellpadding=0 cellspacing=0><tr><td>
  <fb:profile-pic uid=505543152></fb:profile-pic>
 </td></tr>
 <tr><td>
  <fb:name useyou=false uid=505543152 firstnameonly=true></fb:name>
 </td></tr></table>
</td></tr></table>
```

You'll notice from the code that we can mix HTML (we've used `<table> </table>`, `<tr> </tr>` and `<td> </td>` to tabulate the information) with FBML (`<fb:name> </fb:name>` and `<fb:profile-pic> </fb:profile-pic>` to extract and display the Facebook data). If you put this into the code entry box and click **Preview**, then you'll see how your application would look:

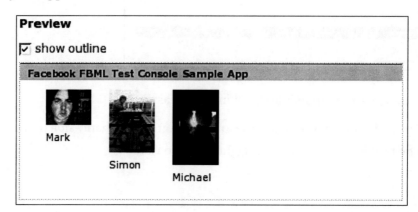

Having seen how we can achieve an output using a mixture of HTML and FBML, it would be interesting to see how you can get much the same results even more easily, by using only FBML:

```
<fb:user-table cols="3">
   <fb:user-item uid="614902533"/>
   <fb:user-item uid="286603790"/>
   <fb:user-item uid="505543152"/>
   <fb:user-item uid="515482742"/>
   <fb:user-item uid="517311956"/>
   <fb:user-item uid="521240370"/>
</fb:user-table>
```

You can see from the code that we're able to use the FBML `<fb:user-table>` tag to create a table, and we've used the `<fb:user-item>` tag to obtain the information that we want from Facebook. The resulting application would look like this:

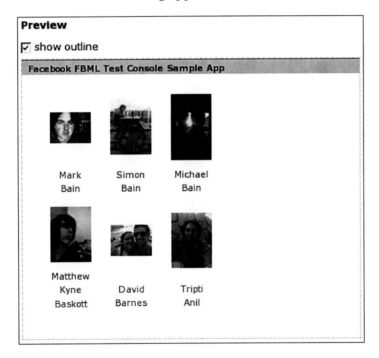

We've looked at the Facebook API and FBML, and learned how useful they can be. Now, we'll move on to the potentially most powerful element of the Facebook platform—FQL.

FQL

It may interest you to know that the information that you can obtain from Facebook is actually stored in a database, and that's where FQL comes in. So, instead of using the API methods, we can query the tables in the database to obtain the information that we require. For example, if you want the first name, surname, and birthday of each of your friends, then you can use the following query in the API Test Console:

```
SELECT first_name, last_name,birthday
FROM user
WHERE uid IN (    SELECT uid1
                  FROM friend
                  WHERE uid2=614902533)
```

And don't forget to replace my id (614902533) with your own because you can only use the details of friends of the logged in user, that is you.

Now, we still need to use the API, but for this, we only need one method — `fql.query`:

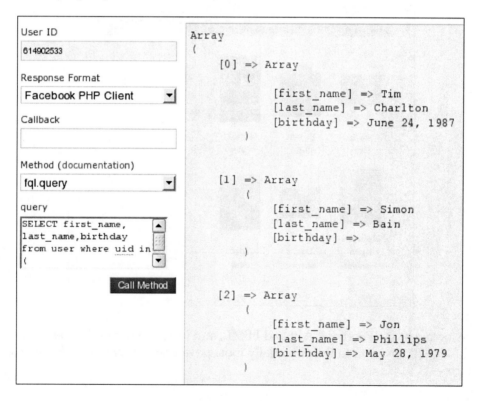

You'll realize of course, that this means that you're not limited to the information supplied by the API methods and the FBML tags. You're actually able to extract the exact data that you want.

Now that you're conversant with the Facebook Platform, you will want to create your first Facebook application. However, before you do that, you'll need to obtain the Facebook Client Libraries.

Obtaining the Facebook Client Libraries

If you're going to build a Facebook application, then you're going to need access to the Facebook API, and to do that, you'll have to download the client libraries onto your server. In order to do this, you'll need to go to the developers' page—remember that you can use the URL `http://developers.facebook.com`, or use the link given at the bottom of each Facebook page:

Once you're there, find the link to the **Resources** page:

Documentation
The complete details on Platform and how it works from the inside out.

Resources
Learn more about Facebook Platform with code samples, client libraries, and more.

Tools
Prototype your Facebook Platform application in real-time with easy-to-use test consoles.

News
The latest info straight from the Facebook Platform team.

Or, go directly to `http://developers.facebook.com/resources.php`.

When you're in the **Resources** page, you can click on the library that you want to use. In this instance, we're going to be using the **PHP (4 and 5) Client Library**:

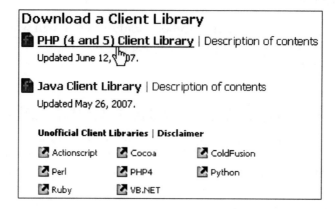

Of course, if you want to know more about a library, then just click on **Description of contents**:

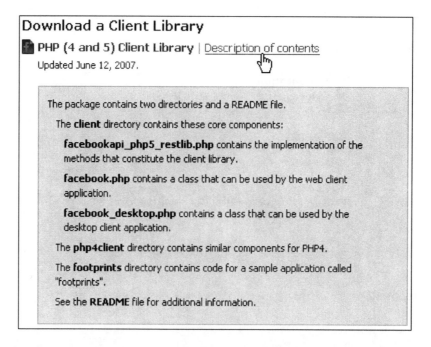

So far, everything we've looked at will be the same whether you are using Windows or Linux on your server, and that's true for most of what we'll be doing. However, this is one instance when what you do will depend on your server's operating system.

The file that you're going to download is compressed, but not in a form normally used in Windows (you'll notice that they have a `tar.gz` suffix). So, you'll need to obtain software that can uncompress the files for you. A quick Google search will find a lot of them, but a suitable one is available from `http://www.winace.com`, although you'll find that it does display some annoying pop-ups, so you may want to delete it once you're finished. However, once you've installed WinAce, you'll be able to uncompress the libraries:

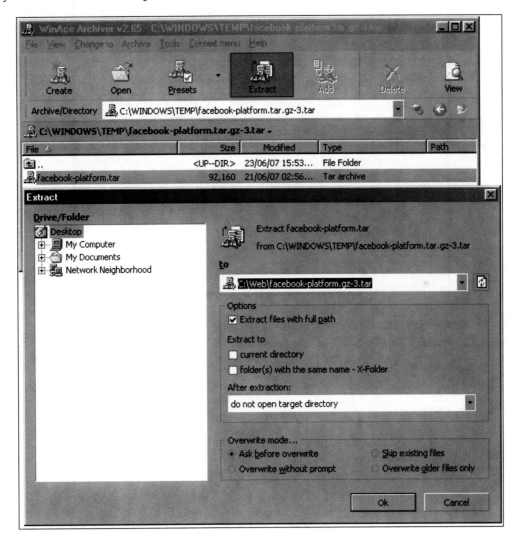

If, on the other hand, you're using Linux, then you'll be able to uncompress the files quite readily. If you prefer to use a GUI type interface, then there is a software, which you can use, called Ark:

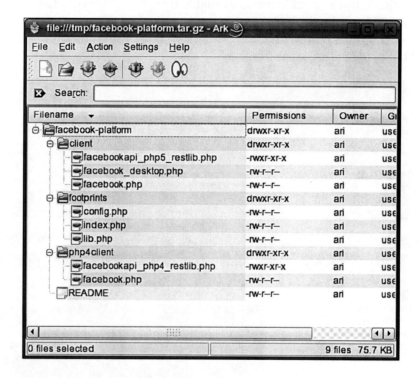

However, if you prefer to use the command line (as I do), then you can both download and uncompress the files very easily:

```
cd /srv/www
wget http://developers.facebook.com/clientlibs/facebook-platform.tar.
gz
tar -xvzf facebook-platform.tar.gz
```

Of course, you'll need to change /srv/www to a suitable directory on your own server, one that you can write to. And in case you're not used to the commands, cd moves you to the directory, wget downloads the library, and tar uncompresses it. If you type the commands on the command line, then you'll see something like this:

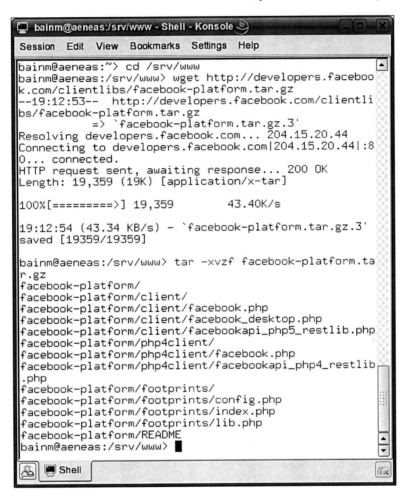

```
bainm@aeneas:~> cd /srv/www
bainm@aeneas:/srv/www> wget http://developers.faceboo
k.com/clientlibs/facebook-platform.tar.gz
--19:12:53--  http://developers.facebook.com/clientli
bs/facebook-platform.tar.gz
          => `facebook-platform.tar.gz.3'
Resolving developers.facebook.com... 204.15.20.44
Connecting to developers.facebook.com|204.15.20.44|:8
0... connected.
HTTP request sent, awaiting response... 200 OK
Length: 19,359 (19K) [application/x-tar]

100%[=========>] 19,359        43.40K/s

19:12:54 (43.34 KB/s) - `facebook-platform.tar.gz.3'
saved [19359/19359]

bainm@aeneas:/srv/www> tar -xvzf facebook-platform.ta
r.gz
facebook-platform/
facebook-platform/client/
facebook-platform/client/facebook.php
facebook-platform/client/facebook_desktop.php
facebook-platform/client/facebookapi_php5_restlib.php
facebook-platform/php4client/
facebook-platform/php4client/facebook.php
facebook-platform/php4client/facebookapi_php4_restlib
.php
facebook-platform/footprints/
facebook-platform/footprints/config.php
facebook-platform/footprints/index.php
facebook-platform/footprints/lib.php
facebook-platform/README
bainm@aeneas:/srv/www> █
```

At the moment, it doesn't actually matter where you place the libraries, but regardless of whether you're using Windows or Linux, you should end up with a set of PHP files somewhere on your server:

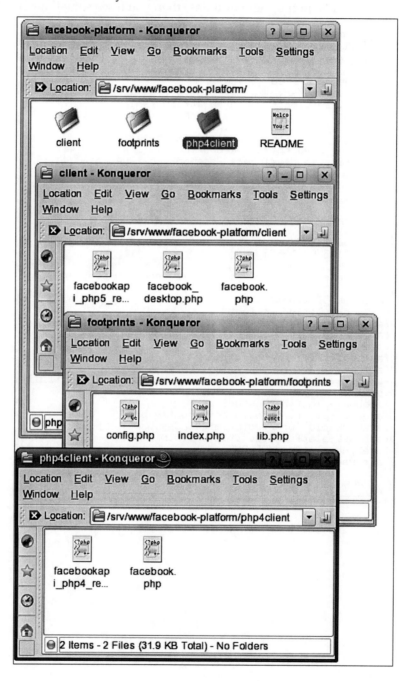

And now, you are ready to move on to telling Facebook about the application that you're going to be creating.

So far, we've spent a bit of time looking at the Facebook Platform—you have learned where it fits in with any application that you build, and you have learned how to experiment with the Platform's functionality, without even having an application. In Chapter 2, you'll learn how to create that first application.

However, before you create your own application, you're going to have to add another application—Facebook's Developer.

Adding the Developer Application

You may be wondering why you need to add another application in order to create your own. Quite simply—you don't use developer to create your application—you use the developer application to *add* yours into Facebook.

So, start by going to the developer's page (remember that you'll find a link at the bottom of every Facebook page, or you can go directly to `http://www.facebook.com/developers.`). Next, you'll have to click on **Get Started**, and then **Add Facebook Developer Application**:

You can change the settings if you want, but you might as well keep the default settings, and press **Add Developer**.

Once you've added the Developer application, you'll be able to access it from your left-hand side navigation:

At this point, you don't actually need an application. What we're going to do is set up our new application in Facebook, and *then* create it.

Setting Up Your Application

If you click on **Developer** in your left-hand side navigation pane, you'll see a button to **Set Up New Application**:

You'll now find that you need to type in details about your application (obviously!). Some fields are required, while others are optional. We'll deal with the required fields first.

Required Fields

Don't worry, you won't have masses of fields to fill in before you can get started with your application—in fact there is only one required field, plus a tick box:

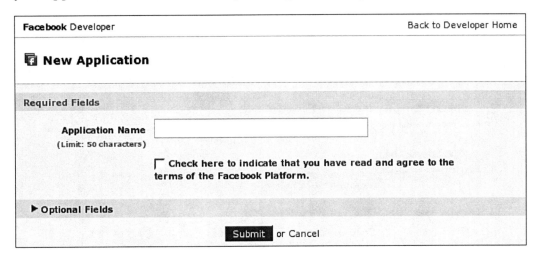

So, all you have to do, at this stage, is choose a suitable name for your application. As this will be displayed on Facebook, decide on a name that describes your application best (avoiding anything rude or insulting). In this example, I'm developing an application for an imaginary private detective, Pygoscelis P. Ellsworthy, so I'm going to name the application Pygoscelis P. Ellsworthy's Suspect Tracker:

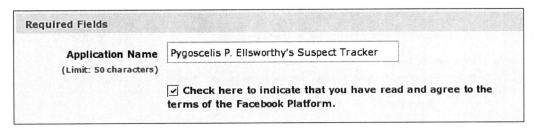

You'll need to tick the box to say that you've read the Facebook Platform terms and conditions (and we *always* read those, don't we?). However, don't click on **Submit** yet, as the remainder of the fields are defined as optional, although some are still essential (as we're about to see).

Optional Fields

By default, the optional fields are hidden, so to see them, click on **Optional Fields** (no surprise there then).

Base Options

As soon as you click on **Optional Fields**, the **Base options** will become visible — these are the options required by any application that you build, although others will be made available to you depending on what you enter into the **Base options**.

▼ Optional Fields

Base options

Support E-mail
(Limit: 100 characters)

mark.bain@linuxtalk.co.uk

We will contact you at this address if there are any problems or important updates.

Callback Url
(Limit: 100 characters)

After logging into Facebook, users are redirected to the callback URL.
See authentication overview for more details.

Canvas Page URL

http://apps.facebook.com/ _____ /

⦿ **Use FBML**   ○ **Use iframe**

Your application will be viewable in the Facebook navigation at this URL - either as rendered FBML or loaded in an iframe.

Application Type

⦿ **Website**   ○ **Desktop**

IP Addresses of Servers Making Requests
(comma-separated)

If you supply this information (e.g. 10.1.20.1, 101.20.3), requests from addresses other than those listed will be rejected.

Can your application be added on Facebook?

○ **Yes**   ⦿ **No**

Select Yes if your application can be added to a user's Facebook account.

TOS URL

The URL pointing to your application's Terms of Service, which the user must accept.

Submit or Cancel

You'll see that **Support E-Mail** has already been filled in for you, using your Facebook email address. Obviously, you'll need to change that, if that's not the address that you want to use. Apart from **Support E-Mail**, there are only two fields that we're interested in at the moment:

- **Callback URL** — The URL of your application (that is on your server).
- **Canvas Page URL** — The URL for your application within Facebook (obviously this needs to be unique).

So, in the case of Pygoscelis P. Ellsworthy's Suspect Tracker, the optional fields would look like this:

And a big tip here — make sure that you end the **Callback URL** with a / (in your code, NOT in the Installation options box), and you'll save yourself many hours of heartache wondering why your application isn't working correctly.

You can ignore all the other fields in this section at the moment, apart from one question that you must answer, **Can your application be added on Facebook?** Obviously, the answer will be **Yes**. But don't worry about your application being accessed by thousands of people before you're ready—in a moment we'll see how to stop that.

When you set **Can your application be added on Facebook?** to **Yes**, you'll find that the **Installation Options** are displayed.

Installation Options

Since we want our application to be added on to Facebook, we'll need to fill in some **Installation Options**. As with the **Base options**, we can leave most of them blank, just filling in a few essential ones:

```
Installation Options

        Post-Add URL    http://apps.facebook.com/penguin_pi/
   (Limit: 100 characters)  The URL to redirect to after a user adds your application.

 Application Description  [                                    ]
   (Limit: 250 characters)
                          A short description of your application, displayed on your "add application" page

      Post-Remove URL    [                                    ]
   (Limit 100 characters)  URL at which you want to be notified when a user removes your application from their
                          Facebook account.
                          Cannot be a Facebook-framed page.

       Default FBML       Welcome to Pygoscelis P. Ellsworthy's Suspect
                          Tracker

                          This FBML will be rendered in a user's profile if setFBML hasn't been called for that user.

 Default Profile Box     (•) Wide    ( ) Narrow
           Column         The column in which your application's profile box should be displayed when first added by
                          a user.

      Developer Mode      [✓] Check this box to only allow developers of the application to
                          install the application.
```

As you can see, the **Post-Add URL** needs to be added (this should be the same as your **Canvas Page URL**), and you can enter some arbitrary text into the **Default FBML** box.

Now, I did mention a little while ago that you can prevent your application being used before you're ready, and this is the section where you do that. Just tick the **Developer Mode** box.

Integration Points

The only field that you need to fill in at this point is the **Side Nav URL** (and this should be set to the same as your application's **Canvas Page URL,** in the base options):

Integration Points

Side Nav URL (Limit: 100 characters)	http://apps.facebook.com/penguin_pi URL for your app if you want a link in the side nav. Must be a Facebook canvas page.
Edit URL (Limit: 100 characters)	 Optional "edit" link displayed on your application's profile box for a user who has added your application and is looking at their own profile.
Privacy URL (Limit: 100 characters)	 Link to a privacy configuration page for your application.
Help URL (Limit: 100 characters)	 Link to a help page for your application.
Private Installation	☐ **Check this box to disable News Feed and Mini-Feed installation stories for your application.**
Message Attachment	Attachment action: The action in the attachment dropdown menu for your application. (Limit: 20 characters) Callback URL: The URL from which you can fetch content for message attachments. (Limit: 100 characters)

All you have to do now is click **Submit,** and Facebook will create an API key for you (you'll need that and the secret key when you write the code for your application):

API key created.

You have 1 key | Apply for another key

☐ **Pygoscelis P. Ellsworthy's Suspect Tracker** | Edit Settings | Delete App

About Page	View About Page	Edit About Page	**Submit Application »**
API Key	322d68147c78d2621079317b778cfe10	
Secret	0a53919566eeb272d7b96a76369ed90c	Once you have completed your application you may submit it to our product directory.
Support Email	mark.bain@linuxtalk.co.uk	
Callback URL	http://213.123.183.16/f8/penguin_pi	

And with that done, we can move on to actually building the application itself.

Summary

In this chapter, we've looked at the Facebook Platform and learned that it consists of three elements that must be used by your application to interface with Facebook:

- The Facebook API—A library of PHP methods that will enable your application to extract data from Facebook.

- FBML—The Facebook Markup Language—used to obtain and format Facebook data.

- FQL—The Facebook Query Language—used to extract information directly from the Facebook database.

Each of the platform elements can be used in the development of your application, but you don't need to develop an application in order to test them out. For that you can make use of:

- The API Test Console
- The FBML Test Console

Before you can start developing your own application, you will need to download the Facebook Client Library, and if you're using Windows, then you'll need to obtain suitable software for uncompressing it.

You have to add the Facebook Developer application. Once you've done that, you can start adding your own applications.

When setting up your application, you must give it a sensible name, and a suitable location (the Callback URL). The Callback URL must be to your own server, and don't forget to add a / at the end of the URL.

When you submit your application, you'll be given an API key, and a secret key. You'll need to use these in your application. Now, you are ready to create your application.

2

Building a Facebook Application

In Chapter 1, we concerned ourselves with the Facebook Platform — our application's interface to Facebook. With that knowledge, you'll obviously want to start building applications (since that's the whole point of you getting this book), and that's just what we'll do in this chapter. By the end of this chapter, you'll be able to:

- Extract Facebook information to be displayed by your application.
- Store information in the Facebook cache, so that it can be displayed on your users' profile pages.
- Store your own custom data.

A Simple Facebook Application

Well, with the Facebook side of things set up, it's now over to your server to build the application itself. The server could of course be:

- Your web host's server – This must support PHP, and it may be worthwhile for you to check if you have any bandwidth limits.
- Your own server – Obviously, you'll need Apache and PHP (and you'll also need a fixed IP address).

Getting the Server Ready for Action

Once you have selected your server, you'll need to create a directory in which you'll build your application, for example:

```
mkdir -p /www/htdocs/f8/penguin_pi
cd /www/htdocs/f8/penguin_pi
```

If you haven't already done so, then this is the time to download and uncompress the Facebook Platform libraries:

```
wget http://developers.facebook.com/clientlibs/facebook-platform.tar.
gz
tar -xvzf facebook-platform.tar.gz
```

We're not actually going to use all of the files in the library, so you can copy the ones that you're going to use into your application directory:

```
cp facebook-platform/client/facebook.php
cp facebook-platform/client/facebookapi_php5_restlib.php
```

And once that's done, you can delete the unwanted files:

```
rm -rf facebook-platform.tar.gz facebook-platform
```

Now, you're ready to start building your application.

Creating Your First Facebook Application

Well, you're *nearly* ready to start building your application. First, you'll need to create a file (let's call it appinclude.php) that initiates the application.

The Application Initiation Code

We've got some code that needs to be executed every time our application is accessed, and that code is:

```php
<?php
require_once 'facebook.php'; #Load the Facebook API
$appapikey = '322d68147c78d2621079317b778cfe10'; #Your API Key
$appsecret = '0a53919566eeb272d7b96a76369ed90c';  #Your Secret
$facebook = new Facebook($appapikey, $appsecret); #A Facebook object
$user = $facebook->require_login(); #get the current user
$appcallbackurl = 'http://213.123.183.16/f8/penguin_pi/'; #callback
Url
#Catch an invalid session_key
try {
  if (!$facebook->api_client->users_isAppAdded()) {
    $facebook->redirect($facebook->get_add_url());
  }
} catch (Exception $ex) {
  #If invalid then redirect to a login prompt
  $facebook->set_user(null, null);
  $facebook->redirect($appcallbackurl);
}
?>
```

You'll notice that the code must include your API Key and your secret (they were created when you set up your application in Facebook). The PHP file also handles any invalid sessions.

Now, you're ready to start building your application, and your code must be written into a file named `index.php`.

The Application Code

Our application code needs to call the initiation file, and then we can do whatever we want:

```php
<?php
require_once 'appinclude.php'; #Your application initiation file
echo "<p>Hi $user, ";
echo "welcome to Pygoscelis P. Ellsworthy's Suspect Tracker</p>";
?>
```

Of course, now that you've written the code for the application, you'll want to see what it looks like.

Viewing the New Application

Start by typing your Canvas Page URL into a browser (you'll need to type in your own, but in the case of Pygoscelis P. Ellesworthy's Suspect Tracker, this would be `http://apps.facebook.com/penguin_pi/`):

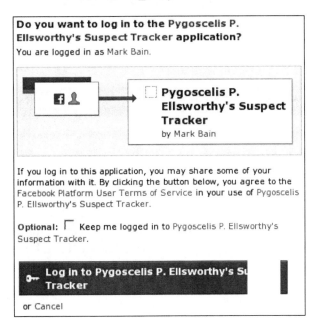

You can then add the application just as you would add any other application:

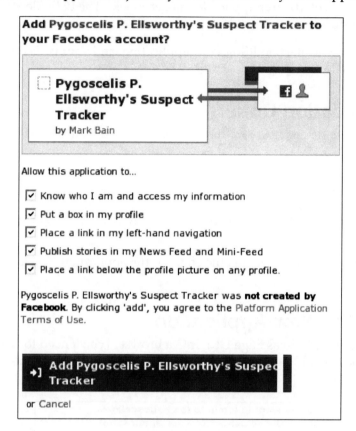

And at last, you can view your new application:

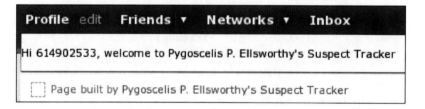

It is worth noting, however, that you won't yet be able to view your application on your profile (we'll see how to do that later in the chapter). For the time being, you can only access the application by typing in your Canvas Page URL. That being said, your profile will register the fact that you've added your application:

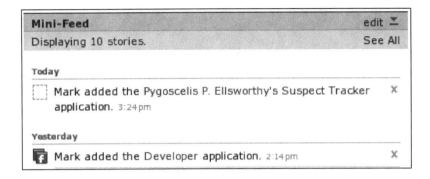

That's the obligatory "Hello World" done. Let's look at how to further develop the application.

Developing the Simple Application

Admittedly, that's not the most exciting application in the world, and certainly not one that's going to get you hundreds of users. However, it is enough for you to see the basics of a Facebook application. We can now look at advancing the application further.

So, let's see how to put some of the code from Chapter 1 into an application that we can actually use. You'll need to edit index.php again, and just as before, start by calling the application initiation file:

```
<?php
require_once 'appinclude.php';
```

Next, we can introduce some FBML to create a personal welcome message:

```
echo "
<p>Hi <fb:name useyou=false uid=$user firstnameonly=true></fb:name>,
welcome to Pygoscelis P. Ellsworthy's Suspect
Tracker</p>
";
?>
```

And mix in some HTML to format the output:

```
<h4>The Usual Suspects</h4>
<table cellpadding=0 cellspacing=0>
 <tr><td>
```

Then, we can use FBML to output the user's picture and name:

```php
<?php
echo "<fb:profile-pic uid=$user></fb:profile-pic>";
?>
 </td></tr>
 <tr><td>
<?php
echo "<fb:name useyou=false uid=$user firstnameonly=false></fb:name>";
?>
 </td></tr></table>
```

The end result is that we've used `<fb:profile-pic>` and `<fb:name>` as well as HTML and PHP to produce a recognizable Facebook application:

Our application uses the `$user` variable that we obtain in `appinclude.php`:

```php
$user = $facebook->require_login()
```

You'll realize, of course, that we're making use of the API in order to do this. So let's make further use of the API by obtaining the list of our user's friends and displaying their details in our application. Here, we're going to make use of `$facebook->api_client->friends_get` and `$facebook->api_client->users_getInfo`. However, we're not going to do all of our coding in `index.php`, instead we're going to add a function into `appinclude.php`. So, the first step is to define the function at the end of the file:

```php
function simple_facebook_app () {
//Define any required global variables
global $facebook, $user, $friends, $profile_field_array;

//Display a welcome message
$text = <<<EndOfText
```

```
<p>Hi <fb:name useyou=false uid=$user firstnameonly=true></fb:name>,
welcome to Pygoscelis P. Ellsworthy's Suspect
Tracker</p>
<h4>The Usual Suspects</h4>
<table cellpadding=0 cellspacing=0><tr>
EndOfText;

//Obtain a list of our user's friends
$friends =
    $facebook->api_client->friends_get();

//and then get an array containing the friends' details
$friend_details =
    $facebook->api_client->users_getInfo($friends,
                                        $profile_field_array);

$c = 1;
//Loop through each of the user's friends' details
foreach ($friend_details as $friend) {

//Now use HTML and a counter to limit the display to 3 columns
 if ($c > 3) {
  $c=1;
  $text .= "</tr>\n<tr>";
 }

 $text .= "<td><table><tr><td>";
//Display the friend's picture, name and city
 $friend_uid = $friend['uid'];
 $friend_first_name = $friend['first_name'];
 $friend_last_name = $friend['last_name'];

 $text .= <<<EndOfText
<fb:profile-pic uid=$friend_uid></fb:profile-pic>
</td></tr>\n<tr><td>
<a href=http://www.facebook.com/profile.php?id=$friend_uid>
$friend_first_name $friend_last_name</a></td></tr>\n
<tr><td>Location:
EndOfText;

 $city = $friend['hometown_location']['city'];
 if ($city == "") {$text .= "Unknown";}
 else {$text .= $city;}

$text .= "</td></tr></table></td>";
//Update the counter recording the number of columns
$c++;
}

$text .= "</tr>\n</table>";
//And finally output the result to the screen
echo $text;
}
```

Our `index.php` file now becomes very simple:

```php
<?php
require_once 'appinclude.php';

simple_facebook_app () ;
?>
```

If you reload the application, you'll see all the user's (that is your) friends' details displayed on the screen:

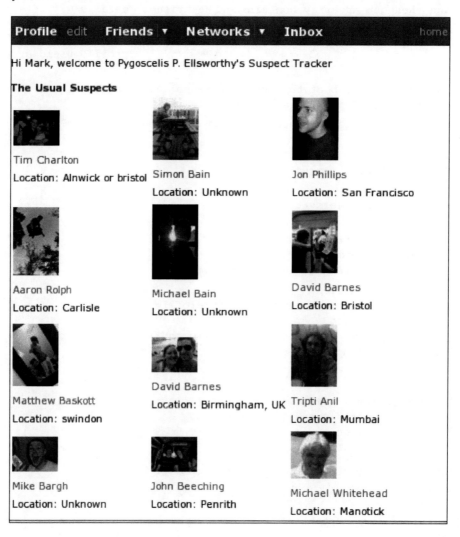

Examining Variables

While writing the code, there may have been a few times you've wondered about the variables that we're using. For example, what is $profile_field_array? Well, the print_r method can help us:

```
print_r ($profile_field_array);
```

And we can now see exactly what's contained in the array:

```
Array ( [0] => about_me [1] => activities [2] => affiliations [3] => birthday [4] => books [5] => current_location
[6] => education_history [7] => first_name [8] => hometown_location [9] => hs_info [10] => interests [11] =>
is_app_user [12] => last_name [13] => meeting_for [14] => meeting_sex [15] => movies [16] => music [17] =>
name [18] => notes_count [19] => pic [20] => pic_big [21] => pic_small [22] => political [23] =>
profile_update_time [24] => quotes [25] => relationship_status [26] => religion [27] => sex [28] =>
significant_other_id [29] => status [30] => timezone [31] => tv [32] => wall_count [33] => work_history )
```

We can do the same with the $friend_details array, by creating a new function in appinclude.php:

```
function get_friends_details ($field_array) {
global $facebook;
$friends = $facebook->api_client->friends_get();
return $facebook->api_client->users_getInfo($friends, $field_array);
}
```

and then calling it from index.php:

```
print_r (get_friends_details ($profile_field_array));
```

When you reload your application, you're able to see exactly what's being passed from Facebook to your application:

```
Array ( [0] => Array ( [uid] => 286601116 [about_me] => Easy going guy Planning to Join RAF when i graduate,
going for pilot. Aim high, fly High [activities] => Rugby, American Football. Poker, especially late night poker at
number nine with an ice lolly in my hand!!! Actually trying to keep fit now. Running has become a certain forte as
has throwing a few weights around, stiil to no avail!! [affiliations] => Array ( [0] => Array ( [nid] => 16780083
[name] => UWE [type] => college [status] => Undergrad [year] => 2006 ) [1] => Array ( [nid] => 67109169
[name] => Newcastle [type] => region [status] => [year] => ) ) [birthday] => June 24, 1987 [books] => Bill
Bryson, Jeremy Clarkson, i will read anything really, hence the lack of obvious authors [current_location] => Array
( [city] => Bristol [state] => [country] => [zip] => ) [education_history] => Array ( [0] => Array ( [name] => UWE
[year] => 2010 [concentrations] => Array ( [0] => Aerospace Engineering ) ) ) [first_name] => Tim
[hometown_location] => Array ( [city] => Alnwick or bristol [state] => [country] => England [zip] => ) [hs_info]
=> Array ( [hs2_name] => [grad_year] => 0 [hs1_id] => 0 [hs2_id] => 0 ) [interests] => Rugby, DJing, trying to
keep fit and socialising with the Carroll Court Guys [is_app_user] => 0 [last_name] => Charlton [meeting_for] =>
[meeting_sex] => [movies] => All back to the futures, Platoon, Ali G, Borat, Blackball, Rambo Trilogy FULL METAL
JACKET! [music] => There isnt a lot of music that i dislike, apart from RnB. I will listen to anything once. Sigur Ros,
Feeder, Foo Fighters, John Frusciante, Chillis, Tenacious D, MJ, Crash Test Dummies, Dave Pearce, Judge Jules,
Hixxy, Sy, Missy Higgins .... [name] => Tim Charlton [notes_count] => 2 [pic] =>
http://photos-116.facebook.com/ip002/profile5/644/7/s286601116_9295.jpg [pic_big] =>
http://photos-116.facebook.com/ip002/profile5/644/7/n286601116_9295.jpg [pic_small] =>
http://photos-116.facebook.com/ip002/profile5/644/7/t286601116_9295.jpg [political] => Apathetic
```

As you can see, quite a lot of information is being passed back (much of which we don't need). Fortunately, we can ask Facebook for only those fields that we actually require:

```
$field_array = array('uid','first_name','last_name','hometown_
location');
print_r (get_friends_details ($field_array));
```

The end result is that less data is passed back to your application (which therefore gives a faster response time):

```
Array ( [0] => Array ( [uid] => 286601116 [first_name] => Tim [last_name] => Charlton [hometown_location] =>
Array ( [city] => Alnwick or bristol [state] => [country] => England [zip] => ) ) [1] => Array ( [uid] => 286603790
[first_name] => Simon [last_name] => Bain [hometown_location] => ) [2] => Array ( [uid] => 500048694
[first_name] => Jon [last_name] => Phillips [hometown_location] => Array ( [city] => San Francisco [state] => CA
[country] => United States [zip] => ) ) [3] => Array ( [uid] => 503027213 [first_name] => Aaron [last_name] =>
Rolph [hometown_location] => Array ( [city] => Carlisle [state] => [country] => England [zip] => ) ) [4] => Array
( [uid] => 505543152 [first_name] => Michael [last_name] => Bain [hometown_location] => Array ( [city] =>
[state] => [country] => England [zip] => ) ) [5] => Array ( [uid] => 511832017 [first_name] => David
[last_name] => Barnes [hometown_location] => Array ( [city] => Bristol [state] => [country] => England [zip] =>
) ) [6] => Array ( [uid] => 515482742 [first_name] => Matthew [last_name] => Baskott [hometown_location] =>
Array ( [city] => swindon [state] => [country] => England [zip] => ) ) [7] => Array ( [uid] => 517311956
[first_name] => David [last_name] => Barnes [hometown_location] => Array ( [city] => Birmingham, UK [state]
=> [country] => England [zip] => ) ) [8] => Array ( [uid] => 521240370 [first_name] => Tripti [last_name] =>
Anil [hometown_location] => Array ( [city] => Mumbai [state] => [country] => India [zip] => ) ) [9] => Array (
[uid] => 690946142 [first_name] => Mike [last_name] => Bargh [hometown_location] => Array ( [city] =>
[state] => [country] => [zip] => ) ) [10] => Array ( [uid] => 705175505 [first_name] => John [last_name] =>
Beeching [hometown_location] => Array ( [city] => Penrith [state] => [country] => England [zip] => ) ) [11] =>
Array ( [uid] => 726195095 [first_name] => Michael [last_name] => Whitehead [hometown_location] => Array (
[city] => Manotick [state] => Ontario [country] => Canada [zip] => ) ) )
```

Of course, we can improve things even more by making use of FQL.

Using FQL in Your Application

If you look back at the code that we've just written, then you'll see that we accessed Facebook twice to obtain data. Once for the list of friends, and then for the friends' details. One of the advantages of using FSQL is that we can extract the data in a single transaction by making use of the `$facebook->api_client->fql_query` method:

```
global $facebook, $user;
$sql = <<<EndSQL
SELECT first_name, last_name, hometown_location
FROM user
WHERE uid IN (SELECT uid1
FROM friend
WHERE uid2=$user)
EndSQL;
$friend_details = $facebook->api_client->fql_query($sql);
```

The end result is that we still load `$friend_details` with an array containing the information about our user's friends, but we've made only one call to the database instead of two.

A second advantage is that we can start filtering the information (again speeding up the application). For example we can change the application to show only the friends who are in England:

```
$sql = <<<EndSQL
SELECT first_name, last_name, hometown_location
FROM user
WHERE uid IN (SELECT uid1
FROM friend
WHERE uid2=$user)
AND hometown_location.country = 'England'
EndSQL;
$friend_details = $facebook->api_client->fql_query($sql);
```

If this FQL is used in our application, then we'll still see three columns of friends, but they'll *only* be those in England:

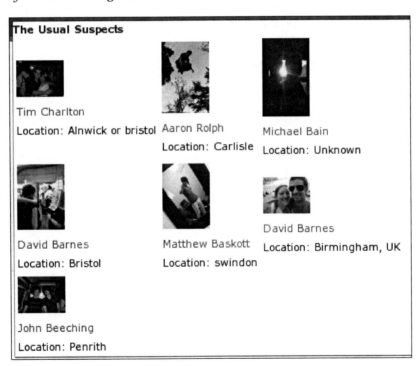

Of course, if you want to be really clever, you could convert the above code into a function, which when supplied with a country returns an array of friend IDs. However, I'll leave that to you. Instead, we'll turn our attention to the Facebook profile.

Here's a question: how many Facebook applications display something on the user's profile page? Well, at the moment, all of them, except yours. Let's rectify that now.

Writing to the Facebook Profile

So far we've only been working with the application page; this means that you need to either access the application via the left-nav panel, or by typing the Canvas Page URL into your browser (e.g. `http://apps.facebook.com/penguin_pi/`). However, if you go to your profile page, you'll see:

Nothing.

And yet this is where your users will want to see your application, so that's a bit of a problem. Well, not really.

However, you may remember that Facebook keeps a cache, and it's this cache that's used to display information on a profile page. All we have to do is write to the cache.

Updating the Facebook Cache

So, we need to find a way to write the output to the profile, and we do this by making use of the API, and in particular, the `$facebook->api_client->profile_setFBML` method:

```
$fbml_text = <<<EndOfText
<p>Hi <fb:name useyou=false uid=$user firstnameonly=true></fb:name>,
welcome to Pygoscelis P. Ellsworthy's Suspect Tracker</p>
<fb:user-table cols="3">
  <fb:user-item uid=$user />
</fb:user-table>
EndOfText;
$facebook->api_client->profile_setFBML($fbml_text, $user);
print "Text written to Facebook Profile";
```

You'll notice that we need to write all of the FMBL to a variable (`$fbml_text`), and that we then use `$facebook->api_client->profile_setFBML` to produce an output for the profile.

You may also be wondering about the last line of code: why do we need to output text as well as the FBML? The reason is quite simple. If we run the application directly (by entering the Canvas Page URL) we'll get an error if there is no output at all. So our application needs to send the FBML to the Cache for the profile and produce an output for the application.

So, all you have to do now is type your Canvas Page URL into your browser:

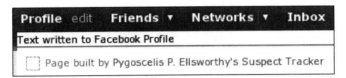

And then go to your profile page to see the end result:

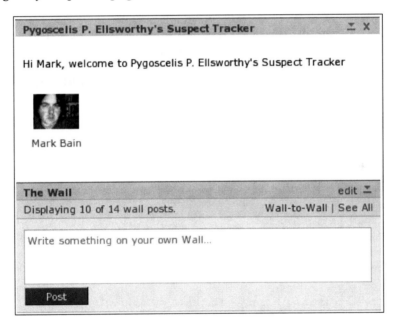

At this point, you're probably wondering if there's an easier way to refresh the FBML. After all, having to enter the Canvas Page URL, and then looking at the profile page to see the effect of your changes does take time. And of course, there is an easy answer. Just change the line:

```
print "Text written to Facebook Profile";
```

to:

```
$facebook->redirect($facebook->get_facebook_url() . '/profile.php');
```

How does this help? The line of code simply redirects the application back to the profile page. This means that instead of carrying out two steps (going to the Canvas Page URL and then back to the profile page), you can now just click on the link to your application in the left-hand navigation panel:

Once you click on your link (and the page has refreshed), you can just scroll down to your application and see the effect of your changes.

And while we're on it, we can also change the code to incorporate some of the work that we discussed earlier in the chapter. I had mentioned earlier that you can write a function to extract a user's friend's details by country, here it is:

```
function get_friends_details_by_country ($country) {
global $facebook, $user;
$sql = <<<EndSQL
SELECT uid, first_name, last_name, hometown_location
FROM user
WHERE uid IN (SELECT uid1
FROM friend
WHERE uid2=$user)
AND hometown_location.country = '$country'
EndSQL;
return $facebook->api_client->fql_query($sql);
}
```

Next, we can create another couple of functions that will write to the cache:

```
function tabulate_friends ($friend_details, $cols) {
/*Tabulating a list of friends is quite useful, and so we'll put in
its own function. That way we can easily use it elsewhere*/
$tabulate_friends = "<fb:user-table cols=$cols>";

foreach ($friend_details as $friend) {
 $tabulate_friends .= "<fb:user-item uid=" . $friend['uid'] . " />";
}
```

```
$tabulate_friends .= "</fb:user-table>";
return $tabulate_friends;
}
function display_friends_by_country ($country) {
/*This simple function sends a subtitle and table of friends to the
profile */
global $facebook,$user;
$fbml_text = <<<EndOfText
<fb:subtitle>
<fb:name useyou=false uid=$user firstnameonly=true possessive=true></
fb:name>
 Suspect List
</fb:subtitle>
EndOfText;
$friend_details = get_friends_details_by_country('England');
$fbml_text .= tabulate_friends ($friend_details, 4);
$facebook->api_client->profile_setFBML($fbml_text, $user);
$facebook->redirect($facebook->get_facebook_url() . '/profile.php');
}
```

And then, it's just a matter of updating index.php to use this new functionality:

```
<?php
require_once 'appinclude.php';
display_friends_by_country('England');
?>
```

Once you've saved index.php again, and clicked on the link to your application you'll see something like the following:

Now, that's all fine, but it's a bit static isn't it? You (and any of your fiends) can see the information that was sent to the FBML cache, but that's all. In this next section, we'll look at how to start making your application a bit more dynamic.

Mock AJAX and Your Facebook Profile

I'm sure that you've heard of AJAX (Asynchronous JavaScript and XML) with which you can build interactive web pages. Well, Facebook has Mock AJAX, and with this you can create interactive elements within a profile page. Mock AJAX has three attributes that you need to be aware of:

- clickwriteform — The form to be used to process any data.
- clickwriteid — The id of a component to be used to display our data.
- clickwriteurl — The URL of the application that will process the data.

When using Mock AJAX, our application must do two things:

- Return the output of any processed data (and we can do that by using either echo or print).
- Define a form with which we'll enter any data, and a div to receive the processed data

Using a Form on Your Profile

Since we want to make our application more interactive, one simple way is to add a form. So, for our first example we can add a function (or in this case a set of functions) to appinclude.php that will create a form containing a simple combo-box:

```
function country_combo () {
/*You use this function to display a combo-box containing a list of
countries. It's in its own function so that we can use it in other
forms without having to add any extra code*/
$country_combo = <<<EndOfText
<select name=sel_country>
<option>England</option>
<option>India</option>
</select>
EndOfText;
return $country_combo;
}

function country_form () {
/*Like country_combo-box we can use this form where ever needed
because we've encapsulated it in its own function */
```

```
global $appcallbackurl;
$country_form = "<form>";
$country_form .= country_combo ();
$country_form .= <<<EndOfText
<input type="submit"
  clickrewriteurl="$appcallbackurl"
  clickrewriteid="info_display" value="View Country"
/>
<div id="info_display" style="border-style: solid; border-color:
black;
  border-width: 1px; padding: 5px;">
No country selected
</div>
</form>
EndOfText;
return $country_form;
}

function display_simple_form () {
/*This function displays the country form with a nice subtitle (on the
Profile page)*/
global $facebook, $_REQUEST;

#Return any processed data
if (isset($_REQUEST['sel_country'])) {
  echo $_REQUEST['sel_country'] . " selected";
  exit;
}

#Define the form and the div
$fbml_text = <<<EndOfText
<fb:subtitle>
<fb:name useyou=false uid=$user firstnameonly=true possessive=true>
</fb:name>
 Suspect List
</fb:subtitle>
EndOfText;

$fbml_text .= country_form ();

$facebook->api_client->profile_setFBML($fbml_text, $user);
echo $fbml_text;
}
```

And, of course, you'll need to edit `index.php`:

```
display_simple_form ();
```

You'll notice from the code that we need to create a div with the id `info_display`, and that this is what we use for the `clickrewriteid` of the submit button. You'll also notice that we're using `$appcallbackurl` for the `clickrewriteurl` (`$appcallbackurl` is defined in `appinclude.php`).

Now, it's just a matter of viewing the new FMBL (by clicking on the application URL in the left-navigation panel):

If you select a country, and then click on **View Country**, you'll see:

I'm sure that you can see where we're going with this. The next stage is to incorporate this form into our Suspect Tracker application. And the great thing now is that because of the functions that we've already added to `appinclude.php`, this is now a very easy job:

```
function first_suspect_tracker () {
global $facebook, $_REQUEST;
if (isset($_REQUEST['sel_country'])) {
 $friend_details = get_friends_details_by_country ($_REQUEST['sel_
country']);
 foreach ($friend_details as $friend) {
  $div_text .=
  "<fb:name uid=" . $friend['uid'] . " firstnameonly=false></fb:name>,
";
 }
 echo $div_text;
 exit;
}
$fbml_text .= country_form ();
$facebook->api_client->profile_setFBML ($fbml_text, $user);
$facebook->redirect($facebook->get_facebook_url() . '/profile.php');
}
```

You may also want to change the `country_form` function, so that the submit button reads **View Suspects**. And, of course, we'll also need to update `index.php`. Just to call our new function:

```php
<?php
require_once 'appinclude.php';
first_suspect_tracker ();
?>
```

This time, we'll see the list of friends in the selected country:

or:

OK, I know what you're thinking, this is fine if all of your friends are in England and India, but what if they're not? And you don't want to enter the list of countries manually, do you? And what happens if someone from a country not in the list becomes your friend? Obviously, the answer to all of these questions is to create the combo-box dynamically.

Creating a Dynamic Combo-Box

I'm sure that from what we've done so far, you can work out how to extract a list of countries from Facebook:

```
function country_list_sql () {
/*We're going to be using this piece of SQL quite often so it deserves
its own function*/
global $user;
$country_list_sql = <<<EndSQL
SELECT hometown_location.country
FROM user
```

```
WHERE uid IN (SELECT uid1
FROM friend
WHERE uid2=$user)
EndSQL;
return $country_list_sql;
}
function full_country_list () {
/*With the SQL in a separate function this one is very short and
simple*/
global $facebook;
$sql = country_list_sql ();
$full_country_list = $facebook->api_client->fql_query ($sql);
print_r ($full_country_list);
}
```

However, from the output, you can see that there's a problem with the data:

If you look through the contents of the array, you'll notice that some of the countries are listed more than once—you can see this even more clearly if we simulate building the combo-box:

```
function options_country_list () {
global $facebook;
$sql = country_list_sql ();
$country_list = $facebook->api_client->fql_query ($sql);
foreach ($country_list as $country){
 echo "option:" . $country['hometown_location']['country'] ."<br>";
}
}
```

From which, we'd get the output:

```
option:England
option:
option:United States
option:England
option:England
option:England
option:England
option:England
option:India
option:
option:England
option:
option:Canada
```

This is obviously not what we want in the combo-box.

Fortunately, we can solve the problem by making use of the **array_unique** method, and we can also order the list by using the **sort** function:

```
function filtered_country_list () {
global $facebook;
$sql = country_list_sql ();
$country_list = $facebook->api_client->fql_query($sql);
$combo_full = array();
foreach ($country_list as $country){
  array_push($combo_full, $country['hometown_location']['country']);
}
$combo_list = array_unique($combo_full);
sort($combo_list);
foreach ($combo_list as $combo){
 echo "option:" . $combo ."<br>";
}
}
```

And now, we can produce a usable combo-box:

```
option:
option:Canada
option:England
option:India
option:United States
```

Once we've added our code to include the dynamic combo-box, we've got the workings for a complete application, and all we have to do is update the `country_combo` function:

```
function country_combo () {
/*The function now produces a combo-box derived from the friends'
countries */
global $facebook;
$country_combo = "<select name=sel_country>";
$sql = country_list_sql ();
$country_list = $facebook->api_client->fql_query($sql);
$combo_full = array();
foreach ($country_list as $country){
  array_push($combo_full, $country['hometown_location']['country']);
}
$combo_list = array_unique($combo_full);
sort($combo_list);
foreach ($combo_list as $combo){
  $country_combo .= "<option>" . $combo ."</option>";
}
$country_combo .= "</select>";
return $country_combo;
}
```

Of course, you'll need to reload the application via the left-hand navigation panel for the result:

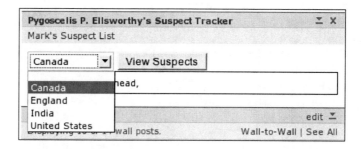

Limiting Access to the Form

You may have spotted a little fly in the ointment at this point. Anyone who can view your profile will also be able to access your form and you may not want that (if they want a form of their own they should install the application!). However, FBML has a number of **if (then) else** statements, and one of them is `<fb:if-is-own-profile>`:

```
<?php
require_once 'appinclude.php';
$fbml_text = <<<EndOfText
<fb:if-is-own-profile>
```

```
Hi <fb:name useyou=false uid=$user firstnameonly=true></fb:name>,
welcome to your Facebook Profile page.
<fb:else>
Sorry, but this is not your Facebook Profile page - it belongs to <fb:
name useyou=false uid=$user firstnameonly=false> </fb:name>,
</fb:else>
</fb:if-is-own-profile>
EndOfText;
$facebook->api_client->profile_setFBML($fbml_text, $user);
echo "Profile updated";
?>
```

So, in this example, if you were logged on to Facebook, you'd see the following on your profile page:

But anyone else viewing your profile page would see:

And remember that the FBML is cached when you run:

```
$facebook->api_client->profile_setFBML($fbml_text, $user);
```

Also, don't forget, it is not dynamic that is it's not run every time that you view your profile page. You couldn't, for example, produce the following for a user called Fred Bloggs:

```
Sorry Fred, but this is not Your Facebook Profile page - it belongs to
Mark Bain
```

That said, you are now able to alter what's seen on the screen, according to who is logged on.

Storing Data—Keeping Files on Your Server

From what we've looked at so far, you already know that you not only have, but need, files stored on your server (the API libraries and your application files). However, there are other instances when it is useful to store files there.

Storing FBML on Your Server

In all of the examples that we've worked on so far, you've seen how to use FBML mixed into your code. However, you may be wondering if it's possible to separate the two. After all, much of the FBML is static—the only reason that we include it in the code is so that we can produce an output. As well as there may be times when you want to change the FBML, but you don't want to have to change your code every time you do that (working on the principle that the more times you edit the code the more opportunity there is to mess it up).

And, of course, there is a simple solution.

Let's look at a typical form:

```
<form>
<div id="info_display" style="border-style: solid; border-color:
black;
  border-width: 1px; padding: 5px;">
</div>
<input name=input_text>
<input type="submit"
  clickrewriteurl="http://213.123.183.16/f8/penguin_pi/"
  clickrewriteid="info_display" value="Write Result">
</form>
```

Rather than enclosing this in `$fbml_text = <<<EndOfText ... EndOfText;` as we have done before, you can save the FBML into a file on your server, in a subdirectory of your application. For example `/www/htdocs/f8/penguin_pi/fbml/form_input_text.fbml`.

"Aha" I hear your say, "won't this invalidate the caching of FBML, and cause Facebook to access my server more often than it needs?"

Well, no, it won't. It's just that we need to tell Facebook to update the cache from our FBML file. So, first we need to inform FBML that some external text needs to be included, by making use of the `<fb:ref>` tag, and then we need to tell Facebook to update the cache by using the `fbml_refreshRefUrl` method:

```
function form_from_server () {
global $facebook, $_REQUEST, $appcallbackurl, $user;
$fbml_file = $appcallbackurl . "fbml/form_input_text.fbml";
if (isset($_REQUEST['input_text'])) {
 echo $_REQUEST['input_text'];
 exit;
}
$fbml_text .= "<fb:ref url='" . $fbml_file . "' />";
$facebook->api_client->profile_setFBML($fbml_text, $user);
$facebook->api_client->fbml_refreshRefUrl($fbml_file);
echo $fbml_text;
}
```

As far as your users are concerned, there is no difference. They'll just see another form on their profile page:

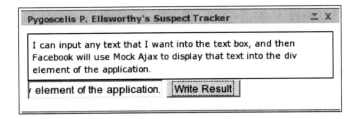

Even if your users don't appreciate this leap forward, it will make a big difference to your coding—you're now able to isolate any static FBML from your PHP (if you want).

And now, we can turn our attention to one of the key advantages of having your own server—your data.

Storing Data on Your Server

So far, we've concentrated on how to extract data from Facebook and display it on the profile page. You've seen, for example, how to list all of your friends from a given country. However, that's not how Pygoscelis' list would work in reality. In reality, you should be able to select one of your friends and add them to your suspect list. We will, therefore, spend just a little time on looking at creating and using our own data.

We're going to be saving our data in files, and so your first job must be to create a directory in which to save those files. Your new directory needs to be a subdirectory of the one containing your application. So, for example, on my Linux server I would do:

```
cd /www/htdocs/f8/penguin_pi    #Move to the application directory
mkdir data                      #Create a new directory
chgrp www-data data             #Change the group of the directory
chmod g+w data                  #Ensure that the group can write to data
```

You will, of course, have to change the directory to one on your own server, and you'll need to check which group your server uses for its web access — because, of course, it's going to be your web server that's writing to the files, not you.

Once you've done that, a simple test will check if everything is set up correctly. We can add a function to `appinclude.php` so that we can create a file in our new directory:

```
function create_file_on_server ($newfile) {
$file = "data/" . $newfile;
$handle = fopen($file, 'w') or die("can't open file");
fclose($handle);
echo "File written";
}
```

As always, call the function from `index.php`:

```
<?php
require_once 'appinclude.php';
create_file_on_server ('testFile.txt');
?>
```

Clicking on the left-navigation link should now test your setup. If there's a problem, you'll see something like:

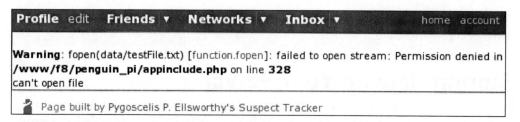

If you do see an error, then check:

- Have you created the new folder in the correct location?
- Have you set the permissions correctly on the folder?

When you have managed to set everything up correctly then you'll see:

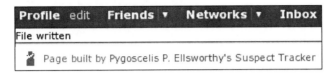

And, of course, you should also have an empty file (testFile.txt) saved in your data directory.

We can then quickly add functions to appinclude.php that can maintain our data files. And the first thing to do is to define a file name for each user's suspect file:

```
$suspect_file = 'data/' . $user . '_suspects.txt';
```

Having done that, we can add a function that will obtain an array of suspect ids from the suspect file (or create the suspect file if it doesn't exist):

```
function get_suspect_list () {
/*If the suspect file exists then load the suspect list, if not then
create the file*/
global $suspect_file;
if (file_exists($suspect_file)) {
 if (filesize($suspect_file) > 0) {
  $fh = fopen($suspect_file, 'r')
        or die("can't open file " . $suspect_file);
  $suspect_input = fread($fh, filesize($suspect_file));
  $get_suspect_list = split(" ", $suspect_input);
  fclose($fh);
 }
} else {
 $fh = fopen($suspect_file, 'w')
        or die("can't open file " . $suspect_file);
 fclose($fh);
 $get_suspect_list = array();
}
return $get_suspect_list;
}
```

Next, we'll create a function for adding new suspects:

```
function add_suspect ($nid, $suspect_list) {
/*With this function we add any new suspects to the suspect file, and
return an array containing the new list of suspects*/
global $suspect_file;
if (! in_array($nid, $suspect_list)) {
```

```
    $fh = fopen($suspect_file, 'a') or die("can't open file" .
                                                    $suspect_file);
    fwrite($fh, $nid . " " );
    fclose($fh);
    array_push($suspect_list, $nid);
    }
    return $suspect_list;
    }
```

Then, we'll need a function for displaying the list of suspects (just to the application page for the moment—not the profile page):

```
function display_suspect_list ($suspect_list) {
/*Display the new suspect list*/
foreach ($suspect_list as $suspect) {
 if ($suspect) {
  echo "<fb:profile-pic uid=$suspect></fb:profile-pic>";
  echo
   "<fb:name useyou=false uid=$suspect firstnameonly=false>
                                                </fb:name>";
  echo "<br>";
 }
 }
 }
```

And, of course, we'll need a function for displaying the form that we'll use for entering any data:

```
function add_suspect_form () {
/*Create the form for entering data*/
$suspect_form = <<<EndOfText
<hr>
<form method=post>
<fb:friend-selector />
<input type=hidden name=add_new_suspect value=true />
<input type=submit value="Add to List of Suspects" />
</form>
EndOfText;
return $suspect_form;
}
```

Now, we can pull all of the functions together into a single function that we can call from index.php:

```
function better_suspect_tracker () {
global $_REQUEST;
$suspect_list = get_suspect_list ();
```

```
/*If a new suspect id has been passed through then add it to the
suspect file and the suspect list array (if add_new_suspect
                                        is passed as well)*/
if ((isset($_REQUEST['friend_selector_id']))
      && (isset($_REQUEST['add_new_suspect']))) {
  $suspect_list = add_suspect ($_REQUEST[
                              'friend_selector_id'],$suspect_list);
}
display_suspect_list ($suspect_list);
$text = add_suspect_form ();
echo $text;
}
```

So, once we've updated index.php:

```
<?php
require_once 'appinclude.php';
better_suspect_tracker ();
?>
```

Then, our end result is an application that displays a list of suspects, *and* allows us to add new ones:

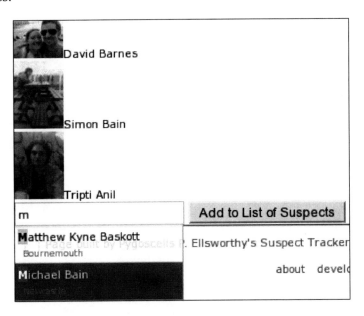

And if we look on the server, we can see the contents of our new file:

```
cat /www/htdocs/f8/penguin_pi/data/614902533_suspects.txt
517311956 286603790 521240370
```

Obviously, the next thing that we want to do is add another function so that we can remove suspects as well. For this, you'll need a form definition function:

```
function remove_suspect_form () {
/*Create the form for removing suspects from the list*/
$remove_suspect_form = <<<EndOfText
<hr>
<form method=post>
<fb:friend-selector />
<input type=hidden name=remove_suspect value=true />
<input type=submit value="Remove From List of Suspects" />
</form>
EndOfText;
return $remove_suspect_form;
}
```

And it's worth noting (if you haven't done so already) that we're using hidden input boxes (remove_suspect value and add_new_suspect) to tell the application which operation we want to carry out.

So, having added a form to select the data, we now need a function to remove the suspect:

```
function remove_suspect ($oid, $suspect_list) {
/*This function removes the inputted id and removes it from the array
(by making use of array_diff) and from the suspect file*/
global $suspect_file;
if (in_array($oid, $suspect_list)) {
 $suspect_list = array_diff($suspect_list, array($oid));
 $fh = fopen($suspect_file, 'w')
         or die("can't open file" . $suspect_file);
 fwrite($fh, implode(" ",$suspect_list ));
 fclose($fh);
}
return $suspect_list;
}
```

It's then just a matter of updating the better_suspect_tracker function to make use of this new code:

```
/*If a suspect id has been passed through to the application with the
remove_suspect parameter then delete the suspect from the list and
update the file*/
if ((isset($_REQUEST['friend_selector_id']))
      && (isset($_REQUEST['remove_suspect']))) {
 $suspect_list = remove_suspect ($_REQUEST['friend_selector_id'],
                                 $suspect_list);
}
```

And just one last thing, at the moment the profile file will not show the results of your changes (to be precise it will show the result of the last `profile_set FBML` that you carried out). So, we need just one more function:

```
function suspect_tracker_to_profile ($suspect_list) {
global $facebook, $user;
$fbml_text .= <<<EndOfText
<fb:subtitle><fb:name useyou=false uid=$user firstnameonly=true
possessive=true></fb:name> Suspect List
<fb:action href=http://apps.facebook.com/penguin_pi/>Edit</fb:action>
</fb:subtitle>
<fb:user-table cols=4>
EndOfText;
foreach ($suspect_list as $suspect) {
  if ($suspect) {
    $fbml_text .= "<fb:user-item uid=" . $suspect . " />";
  }
}
$fbml_text .= "</fb:user-table>";
$facebook->api_client->profile_setFBML($fbml_text, $user);
}
```

Of, course you'll need to edit the `better_suspect_tracker` function so that it calls this code, and now you'll be able to see the result on your profile:

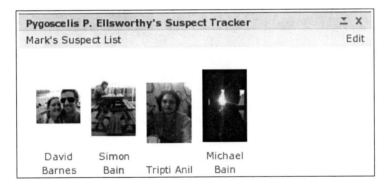

You'll also notice (just to make this a really professional application) that we've added a link from the profile part of the application to the main application by adding:

```
<fb:action href=http://apps.facebook.com/penguin_pi/>Edit</fb:action>
```

into the `<fb:subtitle></fb:subtitle>` portion of the FMBL.

And there you have it—a simple, but effective, Facebook Application. In Chapter 3, we'll be looking at using even more data, and how to get our application to work with databases.

Summary

Chapter 2 has been all about creating your first application—we've seen how to add it into Facebook, and then how to build the application itself. We've also seen that there are two halves to any application: the application page (which accesses your server) and the static FMBL displayed on the profile page (which is stored in the Facebook cache). We can read data from the Facebook database, write to the cache, and store information on our own server. All of which provide us with the ability to create a simple, but professional, Facebook application.

3

Databases, Dashboards, and the Profile

In the beginning of Chapter 1, we looked at the type of Facebook application that we might want to build:

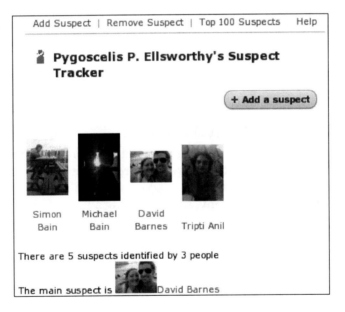

And I'm sure that you'll agree that we already have the basics of a very useful application. In this chapter, we'll look at how to turn our simple application into a more advanced one—one that you'd be proud to see displayed on anyone's profile. By the end of this chapter, you'll be able to:

- Manipulate data stored in a database
- Update your users' profiles automatically

- Track the users who are using your application
- Use the Facebook dashboard, giving your application a professional look

So, what shall we tackle first? Well, let's look at how we can create this part of the screen:

At this point, we could devote the rest of the chapter to developing PHP functions that allow us to analyze the data stored in our data files (the ones that we created in Chapter 2). We could, for example, create a function that looks through all of our data files and works out how many suspects there are (bearing in mind that each suspect may appear in more than one file), and we could write another function that calculates how many people there are who have identified suspects (not too bad since there is only one file per user). Finally, we could write a function that works out who the most commonly identified suspect is.

Or we could load all of the information into a database and get it to do all of the hard work for us.

Of course, before we can do that, we need a database, some tables, and a user.

Setting up the Database

For this, I'm assuming that you have access to a database on your server. If you're using a web hosting service, chances are you've already got a database available to you. And if that's the case, you may need to access the database through the interface supplied by the web hosting company. If you're using a web hosting service, but they don't supply you with a database, don't worry, we'll see how you can use a remote database.

If you're doing all of this on your own server, then you've got no problem. Just install a database (such as MySQL), and away you go.

Setting the Root Password

Once you've installed the database software, the first job that you must *absolutely* do is to set the root password:

```
update user set password=password('root_password') where user='root';
flush privileges;
```

Creating the Database

The next job is to create the database in which you're going to be storing the Facebook information for your application:

```
create database if not exists facebook;
```

Adding a User

So far, we've got the database, and we've got the root user. But we now need another user — a user account for our application to access the database:

```
grant select,insert,delete,update on facebook.* to 'facebook'@'%'
identified by 'facebook';
```

Of course, you'll choose a slightly more secure password than the one that we've used here.

A Table for Our Data

The last step is to create a table that our application can write to. In this case, we're just going to store the user ID of the person adding a suspect, and the user ID of the suspect:

```
create table if not exists facebook.penguin_pi_suspects (
user_id bigint,
suspect_id bigint,
primary key (user_id, suspect_id)
)
```

Migrating Data

Of course, at this point you'll say, "What about the data files that have already been created? Do I have to load all that information by hand?" Well, the answer is no. All you have to do is write a simple script to load the existing data into the databases:

```
FILES=*_suspects.txt
for F in $FILES
do
  USER=$(basename $F "_suspects.txt")
  SUSPECTS="$(cat $F)"
  for S in $SUSPECTS
  do
    SQL="insert into penguin_pi_suspects (user_id, suspect_id)"
    SQL="$SQL values ($USER,$S)"
    echo $SQL | mysql -uroot facebook
  done
done
```

Once you've done that, we can think about the application itself. So the next job is to rewrite some of the functions, so that they use the database to store information rather than the data files.

Accessing the Database from Your Facebook Application

You'll be pleased to know that accessing your database is very simple—actually easier than accessing a file. You'll see this when we convert the functions that maintain the existing data files.

Obviously, we'll need to go back to `applibrary.php`, and the first thing that we'll need to do is to connect to the database.

Connecting to the Database

You will naturally remember that we've just created a database and a user for that database. Now, we need to add some variables to `appconf.php` that will govern how we connect to the database:

```
$dbuser = "facebook";
$dbpassword = "facebook";
$database = "facebook";
$host = "localhost";
```

We can now make use of these in the `better_suspect_tracker` function. So you'll need to change the line:

```
global $_REQUEST;
```

to:

```
global $_REQUEST, $dbuser, $dbpassword, $database, $host;
```

and then we can add the code to make the connection:

```
mysql_connect($host, $dbuser, $dbpassword);
mysql_select_db($database) or die( "Unable to select database");
```

Now technically speaking, although PHP will close the connection for you at the end of the session, it's bad practice to leave it like that. So, we'll close the connection ourselves. We can do this by changing the last line of the function:

```
echo $text;
}
```

to:

```
echo $text;
mysql_close();
}
```

And that's all we need to do with the `better_suspect_tracker` function. It now handles the database connection and disconnection.

Using a Remote Database

At the moment, our application connects to a database on the local server. This is determined by the line:

```
$host = "localhost";
```

If you need to connect to a remote server, it's just a matter of changing the `$host` variable to reflect the correct location. So, you can input the IP address of the server:

```
$host = "213.123.183.16";
```

or the host name:

```
$host = "host213-123-183-16.in-addr.btopenworld.com";
```

However, you're not *quite* done yet. You will need to make a change on the database server, not a big one, but an important one.

You'll find that, by default, your MySQL database only accepts connections from the localhost. This is governed by a single line of code in the database's `my.cnf` file. You'll need to find this file (on Linux you should find it in somewhere like `/etc/mysql/`) and then edit it, changing the line:

```
bind-address          = 127.0.0.1
```

to:

```
#bind-address          = 127.0.0.1
```

Once you've restarted the database, it will accept connections from any location.

At this point, it is vital that you set the root password, if you haven't already done so. If you don't, you will have absolutely no security on the database.

Now that you have access to your database, we can turn our attention to the functions that will read data from, and write data to, your database.

Running Queries on the Database

At the moment, our application accesses the data files three times:

- When the application first loads the list of subjects (get_suspect_list)
- When a suspect is added (add_suspect)
- When a suspect is removed (remove_suspect)

Obtaining Data from the Database

Let's look at the first of our functions get_suspect_list. This obtains (or selects) information from the database.

Now, at this point, you could overwrite the existing code. But if you do that, ensure that you back up applibrary.php first. However, instead of that, you might want to consider renaming the function (for example to get_suspect_list_old), and then recreating get_suspect_list, so that it contains the new code. Personally, I'd do both, backup the file and then rename the function. However, before doing that we can add another function that we're going to need:

```
function get_suspect_list_sql () {
global $user;
$get_suspect_list_sql = <<<EndOfSql
select suspect_id
from penguin_pi_suspects
where user_id = $user
EndOfSql;
return $get_suspect_list_sql;
}
```

As we've seen before, it's useful to put code like this in its own function — we may want to use it elsewhere, and we don't want to keep rewriting the same pieces of code. Also, if we change the query, we only have to update one function. It also has the advantage of making get_suspect_list very simple:

```
function get_suspect_list () {
$get_suspect_list = array();
$sql = get_suspect_list_sql ();
/*Run the query on the database and obtain a recordset*/
$result = mysql_query($sql) or die (mysql_error());
/*step though each row of the recordset*/
while($row = mysql_fetch_array($result)) {
 /*Add each record extracted into an array*/
 array_push($get_suspect_list, $row[0]);
}
/*Return the array filled with records from the database*/
return $get_suspect_list;
}
```

If you now reload your application, you'll see:

So, there is absolutely no change then — well, not in the way the application looks. But now, the data is being extracted from the database, and not the data files.

However, don't add a suspect (or remove one). These functions are still using the original data files.

Inserting Data into the Database

We've just seen how to read data from the database, and now we'll look at how we can write data to it—by making use of the SQL insert statement. Then for this, we'll turn to our `add_suspect` function. Just as earlier, we'll start by creating a separate function for our SQL code:

```
function add_suspect_sql ($nid) {
global $user;
$add_suspect_sql = <<<EndOfSql
insert into penguin_pi_suspects
(suspect_id, user_id)
values
($nid, $user)
EndOfSql;
return $add_suspect_sql;
}
```

We can now greatly simplify our original function:

```
function add_suspect ($nid, $suspect_list) {
if (! in_array($nid, $suspect_list)) {
 mysql_query(add_suspect_sql ($nid)) or die (mysql_error());
 array_push($suspect_list, $nid);
}
return $suspect_list;
}
```

Although your users won't see any difference, all your data will now be written to the database instead of the data files.

Deleting Data from the Database

Our final function, `remove_suspect`, deletes a suspect's ID from the user's data file. We'll edit it so that it deletes the ID from the database table instead. And as done previously, we'll start by creating a function for the SQL:

```
function remove_suspect_sql ($oid) {
global $user;
$remove_suspect_sql = <<<EndOfSql
delete from penguin_pi_suspects
where suspect_id = $oid
and user_id = $user
EndOfSql;
return $remove_suspect_sql;
}
```

Again, this means that we can greatly simplify our function:

```
function remove_suspect ($oid, $suspect_list) {
global $suspect_file;
if (in_array($oid, $suspect_list)) {
 $suspect_list = array_diff($suspect_list, array($oid));
 mysql_query(remove_suspect_sql ($oid)) or die (mysql_error());
}
return $suspect_list;
}
```

Here too, you'll see no difference in the Facebook Application itself, but again, the application maintains a table in the database, not a text file on the server.

Now, we can start thinking about doing some interesting things with the data that we're storing.

Analyzing the Database

We've just seen how easy it is to manipulate the data in our database, and to use it in our Facebook application. We'll now take a look at how to make the application even more interesting by analyzing the data in the database.

So, let's just remind ourselves what it is that we're trying to achieve on the screen:

Our display had three elements:

- The number of suspects
- The number of people who have identified one or more suspects
- The most commonly identified suspect

Now, we're going to create some functions to do all the work for us.

Calculating the Number Items in a Table

You know what we're going to do before I tell you, don't you? That's right! Create a function that will return the correct SQL to us. In this case, we'll count all the suspects. But note how we need to use the `distinct` statement to ensure that we don't count any suspect more than once:

```
function number_of_suspects_sql () {
$number_of_suspects_sql = <<<EndOfSql
select count(distinct suspect_id)
from penguin_pi_suspects
EndOfSql;
return $number_of_suspects_sql;
}
```

Our next function compiles the SQL and queries the database:

```
function number_of_suspects () {
$result = mysql_query(number_of_suspects_sql ()) or die (mysql_
error());
$row = mysql_fetch_array($result);
return $row[0];
}
```

Then, we'll create another function to produce the formatted output:

```
function application_footer () {
$application_footer = "There are " . number_of_suspects () . "
suspects";
return $application_footer
}
```

So where can we use this function? The most logical place to use this is in the `suspect_tracker_to_profile` function that we created in Chapter 2. It's just a matter of changing the lines:

```
$fbml_text .= "</fb:user-table>";
$facebook->api_client->profile_setFBML($fbml_text, $user);
```

to:

```
$fbml_text .= "</fb:user-table>";
$fbml_text .= application_footer ();
$facebook->api_client->profile_setFBML($fbml_text, $user);
```

If you refresh your application via the browser, you'll see no difference. But once you return to your profile, you'll see something like this:

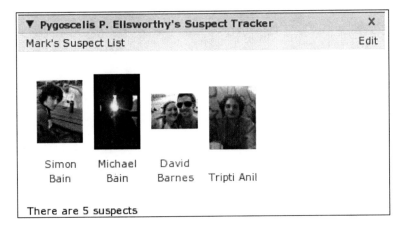

The next thing to do is calculate the number of people who have identified suspects. You'll realize, of course, that the technique for counting the 'detectives' will be very similar to counting the suspects. However, this time we'll count distinct user_id instead of distinct suspect_id:

```
function number_of_detectives_sql () {
$number_of_suspects_sql = <<<EndOfSql
select count(distinct user_id)
from penguin_pi_suspects
EndOfSql;
return $number_of_suspects_sql;
}
```

We need to now compile the SQL, query the database, and return the result:

```
function number_of_detectives () {
$result = mysql_query(number_of_detectives_sql ()) or die (mysql_
error());
$row = mysql_fetch_array($result);
return $row[0];
}
```

And finally, amend our application_footer function, adding the line:

```
$application_footer.=" identified by ".number_of_detectives(). "
people";
```

Next, you'll need to refresh the application in your web browser and then view the result on your profile:

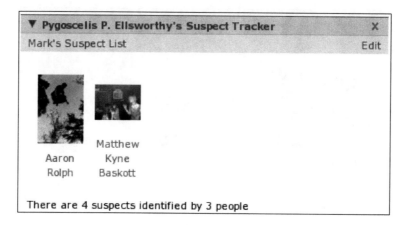

Grouping and Ordering Data

Our last piece of work in this section of the application is to create some functions that will work out who the most commonly identified suspect is.

And yes, the first thing we'll do is create a function to produce the SQL that we want. However, the SQL is the most complicated that we've used so far, and therefore, we'll look at it in a little more detail:

```
function top_suspect_sql () {
$top_suspect_sql = <<<EndOfSql
select suspect_id
from penguin_pi_suspects
group by suspect_id
order by count(*) desc
limit 1
EndOfSql;
return $top_suspect_sql;
}
```

This time, instead of just counting the number of suspects or detectives, we're going to group the records by the suspect_id. This means that we can count the number of times that each suspect occurs in the table. We will then sort the suspects according to the number of occurrences, and then discard all but the first suspect, leaving us with the top suspect.

After that, we just need a function to process the SQL:

```
function top_suspect () {
```

```
$result = mysql_query(top_suspect_sql ()) or die (mysql_error());
$row = mysql_fetch_array($result);
return $row[0];
}
```

Then, of course, we'll need to write some code to produce an output:

```
$main_suspect = top_suspect ();
$application_footer .= <<<EndOfText
<br>
The main suspect is
<fb:profile-pic uid=$main_suspect></fb:profile-pic>
 <fb:name useyou=false uid=$main_suspect firstnameonly=false></fb:
name>
EndOfText;
```

And finally, we'll be able to see the end result in the profile:

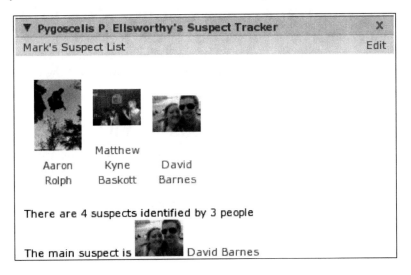

I know what you're going to say now—this is all very well, but the details are only updated when the application page is accessed. What if a user doesn't access the application page very often? How can the displayed details be kept up-to-date?

Well, that's exactly what we're going to look at next.

Updating *Everyone*'s Profile

Let's imagine a scenario. Fred's just added a suspect, Bill. Once he has done that, Fred looks at his profile and sees that Jane is the Main Suspect. He then logs off and does the work that he's actually meant to be doing. In the meantime, Mary logs on and adds Bill in as a suspect as well (by chance, making him the new Main Suspect). However, when Fred comes back and looks at his profile, it will still be telling him that Jane is the Main Suspect. It is only once he's visited the application page that the details are updated.

And you'd expect this wouldn't you? We've already learned that the information displayed on the profile is stored in the Facebook cache, and that is updated only when our application is run.

So what we need is some way of updating the cache automatically.

Updating the Facebook Cache—Remotely

You may be interested to know that you don't actually need to be logged on to Facebook in order to update your (or one of your user's) profile. All you need is the user's ID number and one other piece of information, which is the Application Session ID.

Obtaining the Application Session ID

You'll be pleased to know that you'll have to do this only once. The application session ID is not generated every time you start a session (that is, when you log on). It is a permanent session ID, but you won't find it listed anywhere. You have to write a function to find it. Luckily, that function is very simple:

```
function show_session_key () {
global $facebook;
echo $facebook->api_client->session_key;
}
```

Now, you can call the function from index.php:

```
<?php
require_once 'appinclude.php';
better_suspect_tracker ();
show_session_key ();
?>
```

And then reload your application to see what your session ID is:

Start typing a friend's name	Remove From List of Suspects
ae9fd90d4e323c1603a15c23-614902533	

However, once you've obtained your session ID, don't forget to remove the function call from index.php because you don't want *everyone* to know it.

 If you remove your application and then add it again, you'll obtain a new session ID.

Using the Session ID to Write to a Profile

Now that we've obtained a session ID, we don't even need to be logged on to Facebook to update a user's profile page. So log off from Facebook, and close your web browser.

We're going to create a PHP file, and this is where we really reap the benefit of the way in which we've structured our code. This is where we can use all the same functions, but in a slightly different way.

So the first thing to do is create a new PHP file. This doesn't have to be in the same directory as your application (in fact it's probably better, if it isn't). However, if you are going to be using a different directory, then remember to copy the files facebook.php, facebookapi_php5_restlib.php, appconf.php, and applibrary. php into it (or create links to them).

So, let's write to the profile without being logged on. And, be nice! Write to your own profile first!

Our file (let's call it auto_update.php) starts off the same as appinitiate.php:

```php
<?php
require_once 'appconf.php';
require_once 'facebook.php';
require_once 'applibrary.php';
```

However, here's where it starts being different. As we're not actually using Facebook directly, we need to turn the Facebook debugging off:

```php
$GLOBALS['facebook_config']['debug'] = False;
```

Next, we need to define the session ID:

```php
$appsession = 'ae9fd90d4e323c1603a15c23-614902533';
```

And then, we can use this to set up the Facebook API:

```php
$facebook = new Facebook($appapikey, $appsecret, $appsession);
```

Now, we need to set the Facebook user manually:

```
$user = '614902533';
$facebook->set_user($user, $appsession);
```

Finally, we can send some text to the profile:

```
$fbml_text .= "<h1>You've been tagged!</h1>";
$facebook->api_client->profile_setFBML($fbml_text,$user);
```

Then, it's just a matter of logging back onto Facebook and seeing what affect we've had:

Having seen just how easy it is to update the profile remotely, let's update it with useful information.

```
$fbml_text = application_header();
mysql_connect($host, $dbuser, $dbpassword);
mysql_select_db($database) or die( "Unable to select database");
$suspect_list = get_suspect_list ();
$fbml_text .= application_body($suspect_list);
$fbml_text .= application_footer();
$facebook->api_client->profile_setFBML($fbml_text,$user);
mysql_close();
```

If you run the PHP code, you'll see exactly the same that you'd have seen if you'd just visited the application page:

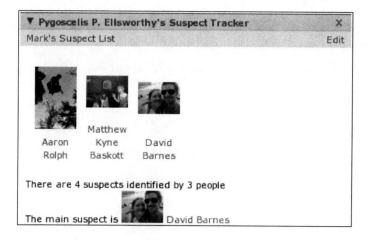

However, here things get more interesting! If you have a user of your application, then all you have to do is change the value of $user; for example:

```
$user = '517311956';
```

and then re-run the PHP file:

At this point, you're probably thinking, "Well, that's really good, but I don't want to update every one of my users manually". And you're quite right too, you haven't got time for that. So, let's look at updating *everyone's* profile automatically.

Updating More Than One User's Profile

We're not going to update *everyone's* profile, we're only going to update the profiles of all your users. Of course, the starting point is to write a function (or an extra couple of functions) that obtains a list of users of your application:

```
function user_list_sql () {
$user_list_sql = <<<EndofSql
select distinct user_id
from penguin_pi_suspects
EndofSql;
return $user_list_sql;
}
function user_list () {
$user_list = array();
$sql = user_list_sql ();
$result = mysql_query($sql) or die (mysql_error());
while($row = mysql_fetch_array($result)) {
 array_push($user_list, $row[0]);
}
return $user_list;
}
```

And now, you can make use of these functions in your update PHP file:

```
mysql_connect($host, $dbuser, $dbpassword);
mysql_select_db($database) or die( "Unable to select database");
$users = user_list ();
foreach ($users as $user) {
 $facebook->set_user($user, $appsession);
 $fbml_text = application_header();
 $suspect_list = get_suspect_list ();
 $fbml_text .= application_body($suspect_list);
 $fbml_text .= application_footer();
 $facebook->api_client->profile_setFBML($fbml_text,$user);
}
mysql_close();
```

With that done, you can look at any of your friends' profiles (assuming they're using your application) and see the result:

Now, another thought may occur to you, "I can update everyone's profile, but I still have to do it manually. Can't I do it automatically?". Well, yes, of course you can!

Automating the Facebook Cache Update

At the moment, you'll be running your PHP from the command line:

```
php auto_update.php
```

We've got a couple of methods that we can use to run this instruction automatically:

- Create a batch job that runs in the background.
- Use the Linux Cron daemon to run the command.

Let's look at creating the batch job first. There are two ways to do this: a simple batch job, or using the Linux at command.

A Simple Batch File

All our batch file needs to do is run our PHP file, wait a little while (say a minute), and then do it all again. Something like this:

```
#!/bin/bash
while [ ! -r /tmp/stop_php_batch ]
do
  php auto_update.php
  sleep 1m
done
```

You'll need to go to the directory in which you've got your PHP file, save this code into a file (and let's call it update_batch), and then make it executable:

```
chmod +x update_batch
```

Then, you can run your batch code:

```
./update_batch
```

This will then run until you either close the terminal window, or open a new terminal and type:

```
touch /tmp/stop_php_batch
```

Of course, you may just identify a problem here—the batch job will end if you close the terminal window. However, we can resolve this by running the batch job in the background (and remember to remove /tmp/stop_php_batch before you do this):

```
nohup ./update_batch &
```

You can now close the terminal window, and the batch job will continue running. You can confirm this by opening a new terminal window and then typing:

```
ps -ef | grep update_batch
```

from which you should get a response similar to:

```
bainm     2475  2403  0 15:09 pts/0     00:00:00 /bin/bash
                                                ./update_batch
```

To stop the process, recreate the file /tmp/stop_php_batch. Don't forget to remove the file before you restart the process.

Using At Command to Control the Batch File

If you've not come across the Linux at command, don't worry; it just takes a command, and then runs it at a set time. For example:

```
php auto_update.php | at 16:30 September 1
```

would run the update file on September 1st at 16:30, and

```
php auto_update.php | at now + 1 minute
```

would run the command in a minute's time. Now, what we can do is create a file (in this case /www/f8/penguin_pi/at_batch) that runs and then submits itself to at:

```
#!/bin/bash
php /www/f8/penguin_pi/auto_update.php
cat /www/f8/penguin_pi/at_batch | at now + 1 minute
```

All you have to do now is to make the file executable, and then run it once. After that, it will take care of itself.

Using Cron to Control the Batch File

We've seen how to create batch files that run our Facebook Cache updates, and there's another way to do it—by making use of the Linux cron daemon.

If you type:

```
crontab -l
```

you'll probably see something like:

```
# m h   dom mon dow    command
```

Hopefully, the columns are self explanatory, but if not:

- m—The minute of the hour at which the job will run.
- h—The hour of the day.
- dom—Day of the month.
- mon—Month.
- dow—Day of the week.
- command—What you actually want to run.

So, if you want to run the job once a minute every day, then you'd type in:

```
* * * * * php /www/f8/penguin_pi/auto_update.php
```

The * stands for 'every'.

Pros and Cons of the Methods

Having seen how we can automate our updates, there are a couple of considerations.

If your system is up and running, the cron daemon will carry out your update. If the system crashes or is rebooted, then the jobs will be resumed automatically. However, if the job takes longer to run than the defined job interval (in our case 1 minute), then you'll end up with multiple instances of the job.

If you use the simple batch job, or the at process, there are no chances of multiple jobs, because each job is resubmitted only when the previous one has finished. However, if an error occurs during processing and the jobs stop, then they will not automatically restart. That must be done manually.

There are, of course, ways to manage this. For example, you could increase the times for updates for cron:

```
*/10 * * * * php /www/f8/penguin_pi/auto_update.php
```

Here, we're running the update file once every 10 minutes, instead of every minute.

Or you could use a combination of cron and simple, have a simple batch job running, then use cron to check that it is still running, and restart it if it isn't.

So, now that we're updating our users' profiles automatically, it may be an apt time to consider just who our users are.

Tracking Users

It may have occurred to you that the list of profiles that we're updating is not necessarily the complete list. Just consider the SQL that we're using:

```
select distinct user_id from penguin_pi_suspects
```

You'd be right in thinking that there is nothing wrong with this SQL. However, it only identifies the users who have actually added suspects; it doesn't return every user (that is a listing including those users who haven't identified a suspect, as well as those that have).

We can verify this, if we first look at the output from the SQL that we've just seen:

```
mysql> select distinct user_id from penguin_pi_suspects;
+-----------+
| user_id   |
+-----------+
| 597432138 |
| 614902533 |
```

```
| 714924135 |
+-----------+
3 rows in set (0.00 sec)
```

And then look on the Facebook Developer application, which is, of course
`http://www.facebook.com/developers/`:

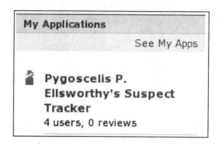

The answer is to store the information in another table on your database.

A Table for Your Users

Now, before you start saving every piece of information that you can glean about
your users, just check Facebook's Terms of Service (which you'll find on the Facebook
website at `http://www.facebook.com/developers/tos.php`). Basically, you
shouldn't store anything that you can't derive from Facebook, and which doesn't
relate to your application directly.

So, what are we going to store?

All we need at this point is:

- The user's ID
- The application ID
- To know whether or not the user is active (we will set a user to inactive
  rather than delete them)

Obviously, the first job is to create the table in our databases:

```
create table application_users (
 user_id bigint,
 application_id bigint,
 active boolean default true,
 primary key (user_id, application_id)
);
```

With our table in place, we can start thinking about doing something with it.

Finding Your Application ID

However, before we continue, you've probably got a question, "How do I find my application ID?" Well, it's back to the Developer application then.

As usual, either go there directly (`http://www.facebook.com/developers/tos.php`), or click on **Developer** in the left-navigation pane. Once you're there, click on your application (you'll find it below **My Applications** on the right-hand side of the page). You should now be able to see your application ID in your browser's navigation toolbar:

You can now copy this ID into your `appconf.php` file:

```
$appid = '2438810883';
```

Of course, you'll need to copy in the application ID for your own application, not mine.

Adding New Users

The question you'll be asking at this point is "OK, I know how to get my application's ID, but how can I tell when I've got a new user?" There's an easy answer for this.

If you take the trouble of removing the application and then adding it again (don't forget that this will change your application session ID), then you see that Facebook passed a parameter to your application `installed=1`. Therefore, we've got the starting of a very useful function:

```
function add_application_user () {
global $user, $_REQUEST, $appid;
if (isset($_REQUEST['installed'])) {
```

First, we need to check if the user has already been added for the application (that is previously set to inactive):

```
$sql = <<<EndOfSql
select user_id
from application_users
```

```
where user_id = $user
and application_id = '$appid'
EndOfSql;
$result=mysql_query($sql)or die (mysql_error());
```

If not, then create the SQL to add the user/application pair:

```
if (mysql_numrows($result) == 0) {
$sql = <<<EndOfSql
insert into application_users
(user_id,application_id)
values
($user, '$appid')
EndOfSql;
```

Otherwise, create the SQL to reactivate the user:

```
} else {
$sql = <<<EndOfSql
update application_users
set active = true
where user_id = $user
and application_id = '$appid'
EndOfSql;
}
```

And finally, run the query on the database:

```
mysql_query($query) or die (mysql_error());
}
}
```

Now, we need to run the function whenever the application is used. We'll do that in the function, better_suspect_tracker (in applibrary.php):

```
add_application_user ();
```

Once you've saved applibrary.php, all you need to do is remove the application:

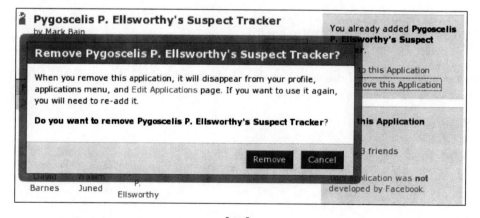

And then, add it again:

You won't see any difference in the application, but you will find some, if you examine the database:

```
mysql> select * from application_users;
+-----------+----------------+--------+
| user_id   | application_id | active |
+-----------+----------------+--------+
| 614902533 |     2147483647 |      1 |
+-----------+----------------+--------+
1 row in set (0.00 sec)
```

Of course, now you'll be asking, "OK, how do I remove a user?"

Removing a User

First, you may want to know if a user has removed your application. Why? Well, think about the update batch job that we've created. If we keep track of who is no longer using the application, we can minimize the amount of processing that the batch job needs to do.

So, having just seen how to monitor new users, you might think that the removal of users can be handled in the same way, that is, a parameter is passed to your application (something like "removed" or "uninstalled", for example). Well, that's not what happens. Application removal is handled in a completely different way.

A user of your application may decide to remove it at some point:

▼ Pygoscelis P. Ellsworthy's Suspect Tracker
Do you want to remove Pygoscelis P. Ellsworthy's Suspect Tracker?
You can remove this application box from your profile or remove this application from your account entirely.
Remove Box   Remove Application   Cancel

Facebook will just remove the application for the user, and you'll be none the wiser. That's not much use to us, is it? However, what we *can* do is get Facebook to notify us when a user does this, and to do this, we need to define a Post-Remove URL.

Defining a Post-Remove URL

So what's a Post-Remove URL, when it's at home? The Post-Remove URL is a URL that Facebook will send information to, when a user removes your application.

To add the Post-Remove URL, we need to go back to the Developer application. But this time, click on **See My Apps**. You'll see all of your applications listed, and next to each, you'll see **Edit Settings**:

If you click on this link, you will see an input box for your URL:

Post-Remove URL	:13.123.183.16/f8/penguin_pi/remove_me.php
(Limit 100 characters)	URL at which you want to be notified when a user removes your application from their Facebook account.
	Cannot be a Facebook-framed page.

The URL needs to be a location on your server. So in this case, we're going to be sending the information to a PHP file named `remove_me.php`. And what's sent to the file? Well, one very important piece of information, `$_REQUEST['fb_sig_user']`, the ID of the user removing your application.

All we need now is a new function in `applibrary.php`:

```
function remove_me () {
global $_REQUEST, $appid, $host, $dbuser, $dbpassword, $database;

$uid = $_REQUEST['fb_sig_user'];

$sql = <<<EndOfSql
update application_users
set active = false
where user_id = $uid
and application_id = $appid
EndOfSql;

mysql_connect($host, $dbuser, $dbpassword);
mysql_select_db($database) or die( "Unable to select database");
mysql_query($sql) or die (mysql_error());
mysql_close();
}
```

And now, we need `remove_me.php` to process the information:

```php
<?php
require_once 'appconf.php';
require_once 'applibrary.php';
remove_me ();
?>
```

Although the user who's just removed your application won't see anything different, there will be a difference in your database:

```
mysql> select * from application_users;
+-----------+----------------+--------+
| user_id   | application_id | active |
+-----------+----------------+--------+
| 614902533 |     2438810883 |      0 |
+-----------+----------------+--------+
1 row in set (0.00 sec)
```

Now that we can track exactly who's using our application, we can turn our minds back to producing a correct user list for our batch file.

Producing a List of Users

After all this hard work, what are we going to do with this new list of users? Well, let's get a correct list of users for our batch updates. Fortunately, because of the way we've written our functions, we only need to change one function to bring this into effect. That function is `user_list_sql`, which now becomes:

```php
function user_list_sql () {
global $appid;
$user_list_sql = <<<EndofSql
select user_id
from application_users
where application_id = $appid
and active = true
EndofSql;
return $user_list_sql;
}
```

Of course, this is another function that only benefits your users indirectly, because it only helps your application to work more efficiently. So let's now look at something that will benefit your users directly, the dashboard.

The Facebook Dashboard

We've already seen that we can start to give our application a professional look by making use of a subtitle:

Now, rather than trying to describe what the dashboard does for our application, it will be much more effective if we just see it in action. So, let's start by adding a dashboard.

Adding a Dashboard

If you want to add a dashboard to your application (just to see what it looks like), then all you need to do is edit our functions file (`applibrary.php`), and add some code to the `application_header` function:

```
$application_header .= <<<EndOfText
<fb:dashboard>
</fb:dashboard>
EndOfText;
```

At this point, you can either view your application (by clicking on it in the left-navigation panel) or run your batch updates. Once you've done one of those, refresh your profile and you'll see something like:

Ok, so the dashboard gives us a nice header and also displays our icon. Is that all? Well, no, the dashboard contains three Facebook elements that we can use to add functionality:

- Help
- Action
- Create Button

We'll start with the first of these—help.

Adding Help to the Dashboard

Let's look at adding the default Facebook help to our application. To do this, we need to make use of the `<fb:help>` tag in our application:

```
$application_header .= <<<EndOfText
<fb:dashboard>
<fb:help href="help.php">Help Me!</fb:help>
</fb:dashboard>
EndOfText;
```

And the end result is:

It's worth noting that Facebook will always display the word **Help**, regardless of what you define in the `<fb:help>` tag. However, if you do click on the link, then you'll see:

Help Topics			
Account Settings	Groups	News Feed	Requests
Advertising	Home Page	Notes	Search
Applications	Inbox	Notifications	Security

Of course, if you think that this is a little too generic, you can change the `<fb:help>` tag to reference your own help URL.

Adding an Action to the Dashboard

You'll find that the dashboard action works in the same way as the dashboard help—except in that the text that you want to use *is* displayed correctly:

```
<fb:dashboard>
<fb:help href="help.php">Help Me!</fb:help>
<fb:action
```

```
     href="http://apps.facebook.com/penguin_pi">Add Suspect</fb:action>
<fb:action
     href="http://apps.facebook.com/penguin_pi">Remove Suspect</fb:
action>
</fb:dashboard>
```

So, this gives us:

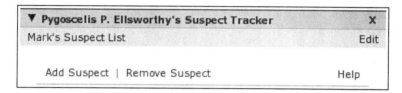

The Dashboard Create Button

As you may have expected, the create button is defined in exactly the same way as the dashboard help and action:

```
<fb:create-button href="http://apps.facebook.com/penguin_pi/">
Add a New Suspect</fb:create-button>
```

But the result on the screen is quite different:

Having seen that we can add functionality to our application by making use of the dashboard, you may be wondering if there's any other way to add functionality into the profile page. So, there is one last area we can look at in this chapter, the JavaScript.

Facebook JavaScript

Technically, Facebook doesn't support JavaScript. What it has is actually FBJS—Facebook JavaScript. This means that you'll need to do some things differently from what you are used to doing. But, you'll be pleased to know that FBJS does give you some objects that allow you to easily add Facebook type functionality into your application. One such object is the contextual dialog.

The Facebook Contextual Dialog

You will have already seen the Facebook contextual dialog, for example:

So let's make use of the contextual dialog in our application. We'll use much of what we've learned so far to produce a contextual dialog that shows the top ten suspects.

As always, it's back to `applibrary.php`, where (as usual) we'll create a function defining the SQL that we want. In fact, we've already got it. We just need to make a couple of changes to the `top_suspect_sql` function:

```
function top_suspect_sql ($count) {
```

and:

```
limit $count
```

We can now use this to find the top suspect, top ten suspects, or any number of suspects we want, and we'll use it in our next function, `top_suspects_dialog`:

```
function top_suspects_dialog () {
```

In our function, we'll load the list of subjects into a variable, and then display this in the dialog. However, we can't use a standard JavaScript variable. We must use Facebook's `<fb:js-string>`:

```
$top_suspects_dialog  = "<fb:js-string var='info'>";
$result = mysql_query(top_suspect_sql (10)) or die (mysql_error());
while($row = mysql_fetch_array($result)) {
 $uid  = $row[0];
 $top_suspects_dialog.="<fb:name uid=$uid firstnameonly=false> </fb:
name><br>";
}
$top_suspects_dialog .= <<<EndOfText
</fb:js-string>
```

Next, we need to define the FBJS that we'll call to create the dialog box:

```
<script>
function show_dialog(obj) {
  dia = new Dialog(Dialog.DIALOG_CONTEXTUAL);
  dia.setContext(obj);
  dia.showMessage('Top Ten Suspects', info);
  return false;
}
</script>
```

Finally, we'll need some FBML to call the dialog:

```
<a href="#" onclick='show_dialog(this);return false;'>
Top Ten Suspects</a>
EndOfText;
return $top_suspects_dialog;
}
```

We'll also need to add some code to our `application_header` function:

```
$application_header .= top_suspects_dialog ();
```

And our end result is:

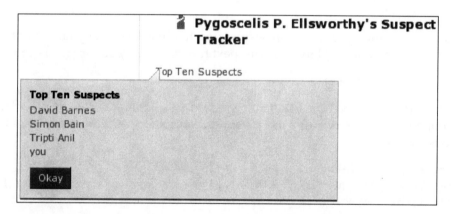

Admittedly, there are only four suspects here. But in Chapter 4, we'll start looking at ways in which we can improve on this by increasing our user base.

Summary

In this chapter, we've seen how to make the most of our data by storing it in a database, rather than as a set of files. We've seen how to select, insert, update, and delete data—all defined in PHP functions. We have also looked at methods of updating multiple users' profiles remotely and automatically, after finding the application's session ID.

We have learnt that we can track who's installed our application by making use of Facebook's 'installed' parameter. However, there is no equivalent for users who uninstall the application. For this, you must define a Post-Remove URL. Facebook will then send the ID of the user to your URL, allowing you to process the data (and all of this is invisible to the user).

Next, we looked at the Facebook dashboard, and saw that it consists of Three elements—help, action, and the create button. And finally, we saw that we can't use JavaScript in our application, but can use Facebook JavaScript instead.

4
Cooking User Data

The core of social networking applications such as Facebook, Linked In, hi5, and Orkut, are the users. These applications have no meaning at all unless they have millions of users who are creating networks, sharing their data, and interacting with one another. So when you develop applications or widgets for these platforms, one of the major concerns is to collect user data, and deal with it. Facebook, being an excellent platform for application developers, provides some REST-based APIs to fetch user data easily. In this chapter, we will discuss in detail how we can fetch the information and make use of those in our applications. Though Facebook provides their APIs as REST API, you don't have to worry much about it, because there is also a wrapper library for PHP developers, which is available from Facebook. So, let's start having fun with user data.

How to Fetch User Data

Facebook provides three different ways to access user data. You can use whichever one you want, depending on your need.

The first one is via FBML. This is mainly used for displaying user data in application. FBML provides a set of tags where you have to pass the user ID to display other data relevant to that user. FBML is directly processed by Facebook after your PHP script finishes execution, and outputs the FBML code to the client. So if you want to manipulate this data inside your PHP script, you have to use FQL or Facebook REST APIs.

Next, is FQL, which stands for Facebook Query Language and works almost like a standard SQL query. But, Facebook lets you access only specific tables via FQL. The access is strictly restricted, so you can access only your data and your friends'. Facebook will not allow accessing confidential user data such as email addresses and phone numbers, which would be a violation of privacy.

The third and comparatively easier one is retrieving data via the Facebook API client library, which actually makes REST calls to Facebook, and returns data as an array. All the data that you can retrieve via the client library is also retrievable by FQL statements. For merging subsequent calls into one, you can sometimes use FQL instead of an API call, which will be better in performance.

In this chapter, we will go through FQL, FBML, and REST library and learn how to use them. Just to remind you, FQL is more for programming and FBML is more for presenting. Let's start with FBML.

FBML

The easiest way for Facebook application developers to display user-specific data in their applications is to use FBML. Sometimes, it is not even possible to access certain data without FBML. For example, you cannot access user network data using API. If you ever used JSTL, you will find that FBML is something similar to that. FBML is totally tag-based, and these FBML tags require user IDs to pass to them as the primary parameter. Besides this default parameter, most of these tags accept a range of optional parameters to make decisions and display data, accordingly. As long as you have a user ID in your hand, you can display some nicely formatted and easily fetched data to the users of these applications. Let's take a look at them, one by one.

You can check all FBML tags instantly using the tool provided by Facebook. Just point your browser to `http://developers.facebook.com/tools.php?fbml`.

fb:name

This tag helps you to display the user's name in a nice format. The primary parameter to pass to this tag is `uid`, which means user ID. For example:

```
<fb:name uid='503274632' />
```

will display "Hasin Hayder" (the name of the user with that ID). There are other parameters to display the name in other formats:

```
<fb:name uid='503274632' linked='true' />
```

will display the user name as a hyperlink to his or her profile page.

```
<fb:name uid='503274632' reflexive='true' /> if "useyou"
```

will display "yourself".

```
<fb:name uid='503274632' possessive='true' />
```

will display the name as a possessive one. So, if you write your user ID (and set `useyou` as `true`), you will see *yours* instead of *you*. For example, if the user's name is **David**, you will see **David's** as the output, when possessive is set to true.

```
<fb:name uid='503274632' shownetwork='true' />
```

will display the primary network for that user beside his or her name. The output will look like Username (Network). If the user doesn't belong to any network, "(no network)" will be displayed beside his name.

```
<fb:name uid='503274632' capitalize='true' />
```

will display the username in capitals.

```
<fb:name uid='503274632' useyou='true' />
```

If `useyou` is set to true, then the logged in user will see *you* as his or her name, when they are logged on. Otherwise, the user's name will be displayed.

There is another optional parameter called `subjectid`, which is the ID of the subject of the sentence. When `subjectid` is used, `uid` is considered to be the object, and `uid`'s name is produced.

fb:pronoun

This is another interesting FBML tag used to display the correct pronoun for a user. For example, you cannot display **he** or **she,** and **his** or **her** properly without knowing the user's gender. Facebook will internally take care of it and display the right one for that user.

```
<fb:pronoun uid='503274632' />
```

will display **he** or **she** depending on the gender of that user. If no gender is specified, it will display **they**.

```
<fb:pronoun uid='503274632' useyou= 'true' />
```

will display **you** if the user who is viewing this application and the supplied user ID are the same.

```
<fb:pronoun uid='503274632' possessive='true' />
```

will display his/her/your/their, depending on gender.

```
<fb:pronoun uid='503274632' reflexive= 'true' />
```

will display himself/herself/themselves/yourself, depending on gender and the user.

```
<fb:pronoun uid='503274632' capitalize='true' />
```

will display the pronoun in capital letters.

```
<fb:pronoun uid='503274632' usethey='true' />
```

will display the pronoun,"they", if no gender is specified.

```
<fb:pronoun uid='503274632' objective='true' />
```

will display pronoun in objective form, such as you/him/her/them.

Let's take a look at the following FBML code:

```
<fb:name useyou= 'false' uid= '503274632' linked= 'true' /> Has 88
Friends. You can invite <fb:pronoun uid= '503274632' useyou= 'false'
objective= 'true' /> as your Friend
```

This will display:

<a href="http://www.facebook.com/profile.php?id=503274632" onclick="(new Image()).src = '/ajax/ct.php?app_id=2353941073&action_type=3&post_form_i d=12a0d59907403fae6a40734cae08acdb&position=2&' + Math.random();return true;">Hasin Hayder</a> Has 88 Friends. You can invite him as your Friend

fb:profile-pic

This FBML tag helps application developers to display the profile picture of any user (if the viewer is allowed to see it, which depends on the user's privacy settings) in four different sizes. While displaying user pictures, you can even link them to the user's profile page.

```
<fb:profile-pic uid='503274632' >
```

will display a user's profile picture as a thumbnail.

```
<fb:profile-pic linked= 'true' uid='503274632' >
```

will display a user's profile picture as a thumbnail, but hyperlinked to that user's profile page. By default, this is set to true.

```
<fb:profile-pic size= 'square' uid='503274632' >
```

will display a user's profile picture as a 50 X 50 pixel square image. There are three other possible values you can set for size: **thumb**, **small**, and **normal**. When you set the size as **normal**, it will display the picture as a 100px wide image, preserving the aspect ratio. The width for **normal** is 200px wide. Take a look at the following screenshot, which demonstrates this tag:

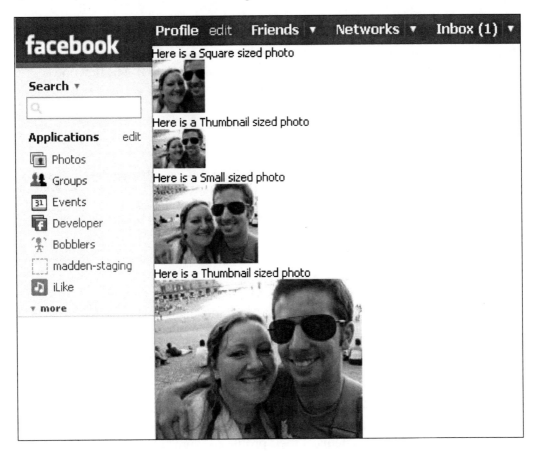

fb:user

This is actually a logical FBML tag that first checks if the viewer is allowed to see this user. If positive, it will render the content inside this tag, otherwise, it keeps the data unseen.

```
<fb:user uid= '503274632'>
    Some data you can see only if you really can see me.
</fb:user>
```

So the user will be able to see only the enclosed data that is specified by this user ID.

Logical Tags

Besides the above tags, there are some logical tags that relate closely to user-specific data, and help Facebook application developers to represent information based on those. These are logical FBML tags. In this section, we will see how to use them.

fb:is-in-network

This tag helps an application developer to decide if a user belongs to any specific network. To make it work, you need to pass two parameters to it. The first one is user ID (`uid`) and the second one is a network ID.

```
<fb:is-in-network network= '' uid= '' >
   <fb:name uid= ''> belongs to Bangladesh network
</fb:is-in-network>
```

Now, if the user belongs to the specified network (in this case, Bangladesh), then the viewer will see: **User Name belongs to Bangladesh network**.

You can also use the `<fb:else>` tag with it. The else tag will be rendered, if the user doesn't belong to the specific network.

```
<fb:is-in-network network= '' uid= '' >
   <fb:name uid= ''> belongs to Bangladesh network
   <fb:else>
      <fb:name uid= ''> belongs to Bangladesh network
   </fb:else>
</fb:is-in-network>
```

fb:if-can-see

This is another very interesting FBML tag that helps application developers maintain the proper level of privacy for a specific user. To help you understand, Facebook allows users to specify which items of their profile are viewable by the public or by their friends. So if Mr. X doesn't want to display his feed data to Mr. Y, then you should also maintain that level of privacy in your application so that you are not displaying any feed-related data of Mr X to Mr.Y.

This can be done easily with the help of this FBML tag. This tag needs two parameters to work properly. The first one is the user ID and the second one is the item that you want to make your decision on. Let's see how:

```
<fb:if-can-see uid= '' what= 'profile' >
   Yes, you are seeing this data because my profile is viewable
                                                      to you.
</fb:if-can-see>
```

Now, if the viewer has the permission to see the profile of the user, which we supplied to this tag as uid, then he will be able to see the enclosed content. You can also use <fb:else> tag to display alternate content, if the viewer is not allowed to see that specific content.

You can supply the following items as what parameters:

```
profile, friends, not_limited, online, statusupdates, wall,
groups, courses, photosofme, notes, feed, contact, email, aim, cell,
phone, mailbox, address, basic, education, professional, personal
and seasonal
```

fb:if-can-see-photo

This tag is used to determine if the logged in user is able to view a specific photo. And based on that decision, the enclosed content will be rendered to the viewer. You can find the ID of a photo from the URL of that photo. For example, look at the following URL:

```
http://www.facebook.com/photo.php?pid=109578&id=503274632
```

You can write FBML like this:

```
<fb:if-can-see-photo uid= '503274632' pid= '109578'>
    <fb:photo pid="109578" />
</fb:if-can-see-photo>
```

If you don't see the content, try the above code by replacing the userid to someone in your network.

This code block will display the photo, if the viewer has the right to view that photo. You can also display alternate contents using <fb:else> instead of showing blank content, when a user has no right to view that photo.

fb: if-is-friends-with-viewer

This tag renders the enclosed content accessible if the supplied user ID is in the friend list of the viewer. Otherwise, you can render the content using the <fb:else> tag. The required parameter is user ID.

```
<fb:if-is-friends-with-viewer uid= '' >
Some content to display
</ fb:if-is-friends-with-viewer>
```

There is one more parameter supported by this tag which is includeself. If the supplied user ID and viewer are the same, it will display the content inside the block, if this parameter is set to true.

fb:is-if-group-member

This FBML tags helps you determine if a specific user is a member of a particular group. You can even check the role of that user in that group, and display the data accordingly. This tag supports three parameters, which are, gid or group ID, uid as in user ID, and role.

```
<fb:is-if-group-member gid= '' uid= '' >
Hey, <fb:name uid = '' /> is the member of this group
</fb:is-if-group-member>
```

With the optional role parameter, you can check the role of that user. You can supply three supported values to this parameter: admin, member, and officer.

```
<fb:is-if-group-member gid= '' uid= '' role= 'admin' >
Hey, <fb:name uid = '' /> is the Admin of this group
</fb:is-if-group-member>
```

fb:is-own-profile

What if you want to display some content and the viewer is the owner of that profile? This FBML tag will come in handy because it allows rendering the enclosed content to the viewer, if he is the owner of that profile page.

```
<fb:is-own-profile uid = '' >
   Data available to you if you are viewing it in your own profile.
</fb:is-own-profile>
```

You can also use the <fb:else> tag with it.

fb:if-is-user

What if you are developing an application where you want to deliver some contents if, and only if, that viewer belongs to a group of users? To do this, you have to use the following FBML tag. You don't need to worry about manually checking it from server side codes.

```
<fb:if-is-user uid= 'uid1, uid2, uid3, uid4' >
   Cool, you belong to a special group of users and that's why you are
seeing this secret data.
</fb:if-is-user>
```

There are no additional parameters supported by this tag. And you can also use the <fb:else> tag with this.

fb:if-user-has-added-app

You can use any app without adding it to your profile. In this case, if you want to display some content and the user has added that particular app, this tag will do it for you. This tag will render the enclosed content, if the supplied user ID or viewer (if no user ID is supplied to it) has added this application. You can use `<fb:else>` to display content otherwise.

```
<fb:if-user-has-added-app uid = '' >
Some content
<fb:else
```

You have to add this application to view the content.

```
</fb>else>
</fb:if-user-has-added-app>
```

Here `uid` is an optional parameter. If no `uid` is supplied, it will take the viewer's ID as the user ID.

fb:if-is-app-user

It is almost similar to the previous tag. The only difference is that it checks whether the user has accepted the terms and conditions of this application while adding it.

FQL

FQL stands for Facebook Query Language, which is almost similar to the standard SQL query, and supports a subset of DDL (Data Definition Language—SELECT) and some functions. These statements look like standard SQL, and you can select data from some specific views/tables provided by Facebook. The advantage of FQL is completely for business layers. Unlike FBML, you can store the returned value of FQL, and process them for sophisticated business logic. To highlight the use of FQL, let's consider retrieving all the friends of a specific user ID, which is possible only via FQL and REST API. Once retrieved, you can display different data with the help of FBML tags by passing those IDs. So, FQL is actually an essential part of Facebook application development.

In this section, we will discuss the schema that Facebook offers for executing FQLs, the different kinds of FQL query structures, and the way to use them in your PHP code. We will also show you different FQL snippets to perform common tasks on Facebook applications.

Let's Have a Look at the Schema

Facebook offers you a number of tables on which to run FQL. But you are restricted to retrieving only the data which is relevant to the logged in user and his friends. So you have to pass the logged in user ID to the FQL statements. There is no way that you can retrieve information of users who are not totally related to the currently logged in user.

Here is a comprehensive list of all these supported tables and their fields, which was taken directly from the Facebook user manual at the time of writing this book. You can run your FQL against these tables and fields.

Table name	Field names	REST API Equivalent
user	uid*, first_name, last_name, name*, pic_small, pic_big, pic_square, pic, affiliations, profile_update_time, timezone, religion, birthday, sex, hometown_location, meeting_sex, meeting_for, relationship_status, significant_other_id, political, current_location, activities, interests, is_app_user, music, tv, movies, books, quotes, about_me, hs_info, education_history, work_history, notes_count, wall_count, status, has_added_app	facebook.users.getInfo
friend	uid1*, uid2* (these are only indexable if both are specified or for the logged in user's user ID)	facebook.friends.get, facebook.friends.areFriends
group	gid*, name, nid, pic_small, pic_big, pic, description, group_type, group_subtype, recent_news, creator, update_time, office, website, venue	facebook.groups.get
group_member	uid*, gid*, positions	facebook.groups.getMembers, facebook.groups.get
event	eid*, name, tagline, nid, pic_small, pic_big, pic, host, description, event_type, event_subtype, start_time, end_time, creator, update_time, location, venue	facebook.events.get
event_number	uid*, eid*, rsvp_status	facebook.events.getMembers, facebook.events.get
photo	pid*, aid*, owner, src_small, src_big, src, link, caption, created	facebook.photos.get
album	aid*, cover_pid*, owner*, name, created, modified, description, location, size	facebook.photos.getAlbums

Table name	Field names	REST API Equivalent
photo_tag	pid*, subject*, text, xcoord, ycoord, created	facebook.photos.getTags, facebook.photos.get
listing	listing_id*, url, title, description, price, poster*, update_time, category, subcategory, image_urls, condition, isbn, num_beds, num_baths, dogs, cats, smoking, square_footage, street, crossstreet, postal, rent, pay, full, intern, summer, nonprofit, pay_type	facebook.marketplace. getListings, facebook. marketplace.search
page	page_id*, name*, pic_small, pic_big, pic_square, pic, pic_large, type, website, has_added_app, founded, company_ overview, mission, products, location, parking, public_transit, hours, attire, payment_options, culinary_team, general_ manager, price_range, restaurant_services, restaurant_specialties, release_date, genre, starring, screenplay_by, directed_by, produced_by, studio, awards, plot_outline, network, season, schedule, written_by, band_members, hometown, current_ location, record_label, booking_agent, artists_we_like, influences, band_interests, bio, affiliation, birthday, personal_info, personal_interests, members, built, features, mpg, general_info	facebook.pages.getInfo

The fields marked with the * sign indicate that you have to supply them some matching criteria. You cannot run an FQL like the following, keeping a starred field blank. To make your query indexable, the WHERE should contain an "=" or IN clause for one of the columns marked with a *.

```
SELECT * FROM user;
```

The query shown above won't execute, because of two reasons. The first one is that you cannot supply a wildcard as field, following the SELECT. You have to be specific and supply specific field names. The second reason is that you have to supply a value to any of the starred fields mentioned in the diagram above, along with your FQL. Moreover, please make sure that you are executing FQLS against the viewer himself, or his/her network. To make it run-able, you have to modify it like this:

```
SELECT name, pic_small FROM user WHERE uid = '<logged in user's id>'
```

or:

```
SELECT name, pic_small FROM user WHERE uid = '<a friends id>'
```

Working with FQL, and results dealing with FQL queries and the returned resultset in your PHP code, is quite easy. Facebook `api_client` made this really simple. After executing an FQL query, you can get the returned resultset as XML, JSON or just PHP array, and then you can process them as you want. Let's have a look at the following example, where we are retrieving a user's country using FQL, and displaying by PHP code:

```
<?
//do the necessary inclusion and initialization to get the current
logged in user
$result = $facebook->api_client->fql_query("SELECT current_location.
country FROM user where uid= '{$fbuser}'");
echo "Country is : {$result[0]['country']}"
?>
```

JOIN as Sub Query

You can perform JOIN in FQL; though it is not as extensive as in original SQL. FQL only supports a subset of standard SQL functions and DDLs. In FQL, you can join tables only via Sub Query. If you want to retrieve the name and uid of all friends of the logged in user, you can take a look at the following FQL as an example:

```
SELECT uid, name FROM user WHERE uid in (SELECT uid2 FROM friend WHERE
uid1='logged in user')
```

Please note that you cannot alter data using FQL. In rare cases, you need to retrieve the name of a user in FQL to display them. If you want to know what the catch is, you will find that the response is rather bigger than usual when you retrieve the names of these users. And you don't need to retrieve names just for displaying, because there is a specific FBML tag (`fb:name`) for this purpose, and you only need to supply the user ID to that. Let's have a look at the following code block where you can display pictures and names of the friends of currently logged in user.

```
<?
//do the necessary inclusion and initialization to get the current
logged in user
$users = $facebook->api_client->fql_query("SELECT uid2 from friend
where uid1= '{$fbuser}'");
Foreach($users as $user)
{
    echo "<fb:profile-pic uid = '{$user['uid2']}' /> <br/> <fb:name
uid = '{$user['uid2']}' /><br/>";
}
?>
```

It will give you something like the following, depending on your friend list.

You can reduce the load produced by subsequent REST call via the Facebook API client using FQLs effectively.

Effective Searching with Structures

Looking at the schema, you will find that many of these columns are actually structures containing a set of similar data. You can select the fields from inside those structures, directly in your FQL query.

For example, the location in user table is a structure containing some fields inside it. You can select only the country name from this structure. The following example will clarify this issue more specifically:

```
SELECT location.country from user where uid={$fbuser}
```

Common Snippets

In this section, we will show some common FQL snippets that will help you in developing your Facebook application easier.

Find All the friends of a User

```
SELECT uid2
    FROM friend
    WHERE
        uid1 = '{$logged_in_user}'
```

Find All Friends Who Have the Current Application Installed

```
SELECT uid
    FROM user
    WHERE
        uid IN (
            SELECT uid2
            FROM friend
            WHERE
                uid1 ={$logged_in_user})
                AND has_added_app=1
```

Find All Friends Whose Birthday Is Tomorrow

To find all your friends whose birthday is tomorrow, you need to find the date of tomorrow first. In Facebook, birthdays are stored in either one of the following formats:

Month Day

Or

Month Day, Year

But whatever format it is, we actually need the month and the day to find the birthdays. So let's get the date of tomorrow in "M d" format:

```
<?
$tomorrow = Date("M d", strttime("tomorrow"));
?>
```

Now, you can use the following FQL to get friends whose birthday is tomorrow:

```
SELECT uid
FROM user
    WHERE uid IN ( SELECT uid2
        FROM friend
        WHERE uid1 = '{$logged_in_user}' )
    AND
        Strps(birthday, '{$tomorrow}') != '-1'
```

Find Which Groups a Specific User Is Subscribed To

```
SELECT name, gid
    FROM group
    WHERE gid IN (SELECT gid
                    FROM group_member
                    WHERE uid = '{$user_id}')
```

Find All the Photos Uploaded by the User and in Any Album

```
SELECT pid
FROM photo
    WHERE aid IN (SELECT aid
        FROM album
        WHERE owner = '{$logged_in_user}' )
```

Functions You can Use in FQL

As we said at the beginning of this section, you can use some function in your FQL. These functions make FQL more usable in complex cases, like the one we just saw,"finding birthday of friends whose birthday is tomorrow". Here is a comprehensive list of the available functions in FQL:

Function	Description
now()	returns the current time (UNIX timestamp)
rand()	returns a random number
strlen(string)	returns the length of the passed string
concat (param1, param2, ... , param n)	concatenates all the parameters and returns it
substr(string, start, length)	returns the sub string
strpos(haystack, needle)	returns the position of needle in haystack, or -1 if it is not found
lower(string)	returns the string in lower case
upper(string)	returns the string in upper case

Using Facebook API to Retrieve Information

Facebook provides a set of REST methods to retrieve user information from Facebook. You can write your own code to make a REST call over HTTP. But if you are a PHP developer, then you can use the Facebook API client library that is freely downloadable from the Facebook site.

Download the client library from http://developers.facebook.com/resources.php. Always update this library in your local machine because Facebook developers add new functions to this library frequently. Also, the change of working procedures of functions is quite frequent. It sounds quite annoying, but if you don't update your client library frequently, your application may stop working after a Major API update.

Facebook APIs related to users are categorized as follows:

- Users
- Events
- Groups

- Friends
- Photos

We will discuss some of them in this chapter. There are other categories like feeds that we will discuss in the forthcoming chapters.

Retrieving Profile Information

You already know that we can use FQL to retrieve information for specific users. All this information is stored in the "User" table. You can also retrieve these pieces of information using users_getInfo REST API. Let's have a look:

```
<?
// do the necessary inclusion and initialization to get // the current
logged in user
//access this page via Facebook canvas url
$result = $facebook->api_client->users_getInfo(
                    array('$uid1', '$uid2'),
                    array('current_location.country'));echo
"Country of {$uid} is : {$result[0]['country_location']['country']}";
?>
```

This will output:

Country of 503274632 is Bangladesh.

The interesting part is that you can send any number of users to this API as an array, and retrieve the result, also as an array. Similarly, you can retrieve any other profile information via this API.

Retrieving List of Friends

This is another important Facebook API, which can retrieve a user's friend list. All you have to do is pass the user array, as we did in the previous examples, to friends_get() function, and retrieve the result as an array. This function will return the friend's user ID as an array:

```
<?
//do the necessary inclusion and initialization to get the current
logged in user
//access this page via Facebook canvas url
$result = $facebook->api_client->friends_get(array('503274632'));
echo "<pre>";
print_r($result);
echo "</pre>";
?>
```

This will print out the IDs of all the friends of the corresponding user.

Finding Out If Some Users are Friends

The `Friends_areFriends` method can figure out if some users are friends with each other. This function takes two arrays of users and matches the cardinals of one array to another to check if they are friends. For example if you pass two arrays like this; array(a,b,c) and array(e,f,and g), then the user 'a' will be checked against user 'e', and user 'b' will be checked against user 'f', and so on. The result will contain three arrays which tells us if 'a' and 'e' are friends, 'b' and 'f' are friends, and finally, if 'd' and 'g' are friends with each other.

```
<?
//do the necessary inclusion and initialization to get the current
logged in user
//access this page via Facebook canvas url
$result = $facebook->api_client->friends_areFriends(array('503274632')
,array('1123321'));
Foreach($result as $data){
$friend = $data[are_friends]==true? "is friend": "is not friend";
echo "<fb:name uid= '{$data['uid1']}' /> {$friend} with <fb:name uid=
'{$data['uid2']}' />
}
?>
```

Retrieving Group Member's Information

The `Groups_getMembers` API will return detailed information about a specific group. The users of that group will be returned in four categories: members, admins, officers, and not_replied lists. The members list also contains the members from the admins and the officers group, but not from the not_replied group. The following code will help you understand this:

```
<?
//do the necessary inclusion and initialization to get the current
logged in user
//access this page via Facebook canvas url
$result = $facebook->api_client->groups_getMembers('2260940324');
echo "<pre>";
print_r($result);
echo "</pre>";
?>
```

The code above will output the following array:

```
Array
(
    [members] => Array
```

```
                (
                        [0]  =>  90403625
                        [1]  =>  500293690
                        [2]  =>  500488757
                        [3]  =>  500580112
                        [4]  =>  503274632
                        [5]  =>  530925121
                        [6]  =>  539297661
                )
        [admins]  =>  Array
                (
                        [0]  =>  530925121
                )
        [officers]  =>  Array
                (
                        [0]  =>  539297661
                )
        [not_replied]  =>  Array
                (
                        [0]  =>  504424763
                )

)
```

Retrieving a User's Photo

Photos in Facebook are stored under albums. So, to retrieve the photo of a particular user, you have to retrieve all the albums that belong to the user first. Once you have done this, you have to fetch all the photos that belong to those albums. If you use FQL, you can do the whole thing in a single step, and even more effectively. Let's take a look at the following code:

```
$facebook->api_client->photos_getAlbums('503274632',null)
```

The code above will retrieve all the albums of the specific user, and the returned result will look something like this:

```
Array
(
    [0]  =>  Array
            (
                    [aid]  =>  2161548085346438750
                    [cover_pid]  =>  2161548085346529961
                    [owner]  =>  503274632
```

```
            [name] => Me Myself
            [created] => 1189199787
            [modified] => 1191012279
            [description] => Me Myself
            [location] =>
            [link] => http://www.facebook.com/
                                    album.php?aid=3678&id=503274632
            [size] => 5
        )

    )
```

Now, you can retrieve all the photos belonging to this album, using the following code:

```
$result = $facebook->api_client->photos_get(null,'2161548085346438750
',null);
```

The second parameter we pass to this function is the album ID. You can also specify some particular photos by passing an array containing photo IDs.

The result will look something like the following:

```
Array
(
    [0] => Array
        (
            [pid] => 2161548085346529961
            [aid] => 2161548085346438750
            [owner] => 503274632
            [src] => http://photos-b.ak.facebook.com/photos-ak-sf2p/
v132/93/78/503274632/s503274632_94889_7682.jpg
            [src_big] => http://photos-b.ak.facebook.com/photos-ak-
sf2p/v132/93/78/503274632/n503274632_94889_7682.jpg
            [src_small] => http://photos-b.ak.facebook.com/photos-ak-
sf2p/v132/93/78/503274632/t503274632_94889_7682.jpg
            [link] => http://www.facebook.com/photo.php?pid=94889&id=
503274632
            [caption] => the cyborg
            [created] => 1189199887
        )
    [1] => Array
        (
            [pid] => 2161548085346529962
            [aid] => 2161548085346438750
            [owner] => 503274632
            [src] => http://photos-c.ak.facebook.com/photos-ak-sctm/
v117/93/78/503274632/s503274632_94890_1536.jpg
            [src_big] => http://photos-c.ak.facebook.com/photos-ak-
sctm/v117/93/78/503274632/n503274632_94890_1536.jpg
```

```
        [src_small] => http://photos-c.ak.facebook.com/photos-ak-
sctm/v117/93/78/503274632/t503274632_94890_1536.jpg
        [link] => http://www.facebook.com/photo.php?pid=94890&id=
503274632
        [caption] => Afif
        [created] => 1189200111
    )
)
```

So you can display the photos of the users using the following code:

```
<?
include_once("prepend.php");
$albums = $facebook->api_client->photos_getAlbums('503274632',null);
foreach ($albums as $album){
    $photos = $facebook->api_client->photos_get(null,$album['aid'],nul
l);
    foreach ($photos as $photo)
    {
        echo "<img src='{$photo['src_small']}' alt
='{$photo['caption']}' vspace=10 hspace=10 /> ";
    }
}
?>
```

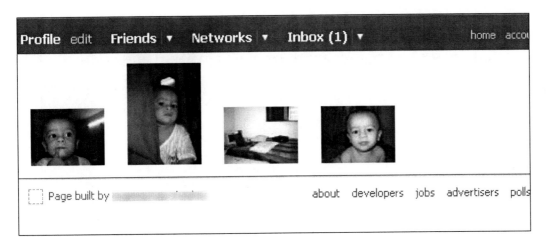

Facebook Developers Tool

Facebook provides a handy tool for developers to test FQL, FBML, and REST API calls online, prior to jump-starting coding. You can get the application by pointing your browser to the following URL:

```
http://developers.facebook.com/tools.php?api
```

If you are wondering how to use this tool, we will help you understand. Let's consider that you are trying to test the friends_areFriends REST API call. So, open that URL. From the lefthand side, follow these steps:

- Choose **XML** as **Response Format** (by default, selected).
- Choose **friends.areFriends** from the **Method** drop-down (please notice that the underscore is replaced by period in method names). As soon as you pick a method from this drop-down, some more boxes will become visible (under this drop-down) based on the required parameters. So when you choose **friends.areFriends**, you will see two boxes named **uids1** and **uids2** have been made visible.
- Type any user IDin **uids1** field.
- Type any user ID in **uids2** field.
- Hit the **Call Method** blue button.

As soon as you hit the **Call Method** button, the result of this API call will appear in the result box on the right-hand side. Take a look at the following screenshot:

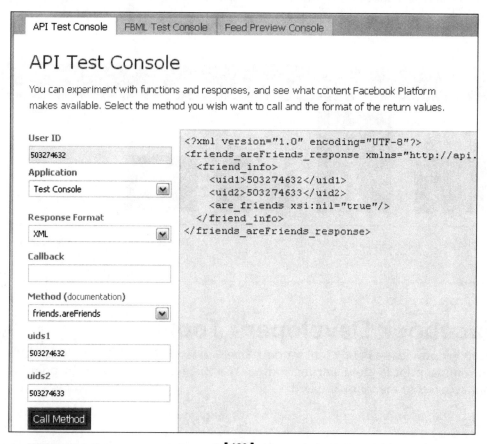

You can also use FBML and Feed Preview (which, we will discuss later) by choosing the tabs at the top named **FBML Test Console** and **Feed Preview Console**.

There is one more thing to be noted here—**friends.areFriends** accepts arbitrary numbers of parameters (array, remember?) in **Uids1** and **Uids2** fields. So you can supply as many user IDs you want separated by commas. Take a look at the following:

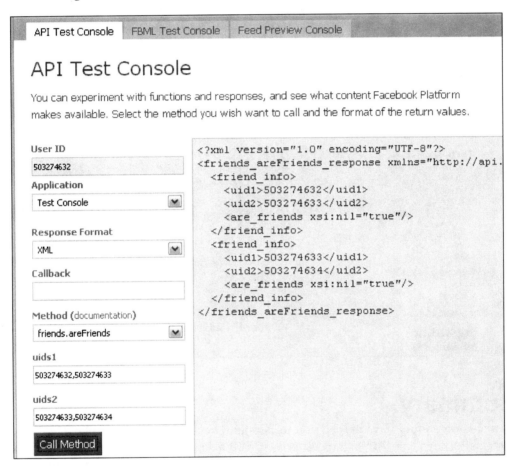

You can also choose **Facebook PHP Client** from the **Response Format** drop-down box instead of XML to understand how the result will look in PHP.

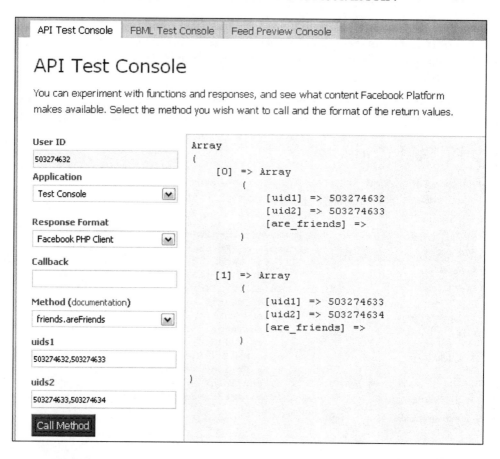

Summary

This chapter should have helped you understand Facebook tags to display information in a hassle free and easier way. You also got an introduction to Facebook Query Language (FQL), and understood why it is sometimes more effective to use FQL rather than Facebook REST API.

Last, but not the least, for PHP developers, Facebook provides a REST API client library to help them in making their application easier than ever. We have also gone through the API and understood how to use them in practical and real life examples. In the next chapter, we will understand the scripting ability in Facebook using a subset of standard JavaScript functions developed by Facebook, which is called FBJS. That will be an interesting journey for sure. Stay tuned.

5
FBJS—The JavaScript

Facebook recently introduced a scripting feature for application developers. This is one of the revolutionary steps taken by Facebook to ease the life of application developers. This scripting system is a subset of standard JavaScript, which is mostly similar to JavaScript, but with differences and restrictions in particular categories. The core difference of Facebook script (FBJS) and JavaScript are in DOM Manipulation, Event Architecture, and Stylesheet manipulation. Though most of the JavaScript functions and objects are supported, some features are restricted for security reasons.

Facebook scripting is called FBJS. In this chapter, we will go into the details of writing FBJS to ease our life, and increase the accessibility of our application. We will also learn how to build mashups using popular Web 2.0 APIs and also, about AJAX. So overall, this is going to be a very interesting chapter for us, Facebook application developers. But also remember that this is not going to be a FBJS/JS reference. We will learn FBJS by creating some intuitive applications.

How FBJS Works

FBJS looks similar to JavaScript. Most of the standard JavaScript code will work without any modifications to FBJS. Some functions and objects are just restricted for security purposes, such as `object.setInnerHTML()`. But there are alternative functions to perform these tasks. And don't worry! That won't give you much pain.

Let's try some basic FBJS to understand how it works. The following FBJS block will change content of some `<div>`:

```
<div id="container" style="padding:20px">
   <p>
      You can click the button next to this paragraph to see how it
changes
   </p>
</div>
```

```
<div style="padding:20px">
    <input type="button" value='Click me' onclick="changeContent()" />
<div>
<script>
function changeContent()
{
    document.getElementById('container').setTextValue('Hello Reader!
Welcome to the wonderful world of Facebook App Development');
}
</script>
```

When you run this, you will get something like the following window:

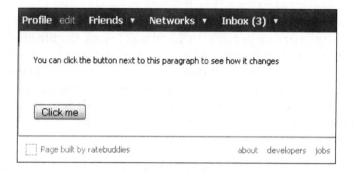

And when you click on **Click me**, the text will change to the following:

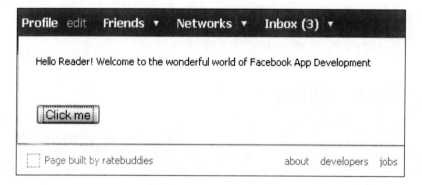

Well that's easy and looks almost similar to JavaScript code. The only difference is the setTextValue() method that comes from the FBJS. This function helps to set text value of any object. In FBJS standard, JavaScript objects are kept almost the same. You can access almost all the methods of a string object, a Math object, and so on.

DOM Manipulation Using FBJS

FBJS is a subset of standard JS. It does not support all JavaScript objects and their methods to manipulate DOM, which is often a very important part of application development. In this section, we will learn how we can manipulate DOM using FBJS, and how it differs from JavaScript. Let's take a look at the following table, copied directly from Facebook wiki to understand the DOM equivalents in FBJS.

JavaScript	FBJS getter	FBJS setter
parentNode	getParentNode	
nextSibling	getNextSibling	
previousSibling	getPreviousSibling	
firstChild	getFirstChild	
lastChild	getLastChild	
childNodes	getChildNodes	
innerHTML	n/a	setInnerFBML
innerText/textContent	n/a	setTextValue
form	getForm	
action	getAction	setAction
value	getValue	setValue
href	getHref	setHref
src	getSrc	setSrc
className	getClassName	setClassName
tagName	getTagName	
id	getId	setId
dir	getDir	setDir
checked	getChecked	setChecked
clientWidth	getClientWidth	
clientHeight	getClientHeight	
offsetWidth	getOffsetWidth	
offsetHeight	getOffsetHeight	
n\a	getAbsoluteTop	
n\a	getAbsoluteLeft	
scrollTop	getScrollTop	setScrollTop

JavaScript	FBJS getter	FBJS setter
scrollLeft	getScrollLeft	setScrollLeft
scrollHeight	getScrollHeight	
scrollWidth	getScrollWidth	
tabIndex	getTabIndex	setTabIndex
title	getTitle	setTitle
name	getName	setName
cols	getCols	setCols
rows	getRows	setRows
accessKey	getAccessKey	setAccessKey
disabled	getDisabled	setDisabled
readOnly	getReadOnly	setReadOnly
type	getType	setType
selectedIndex	getSelectedIndex	setSelectedIndex
selected	getSelected	setSelected
location	n/a	setLocation
n/a	getRootElement	

This table lists all the FBJS equivalent methods you'd need, as against standard JavaScript methods, to manipulate DOM. Here is a nice example taken from Facebook Developers wiki to demonstrate the design of dynamic form elements using DOM methods in FBJS:

```
<div id="container" style="padding:20px;">
    Sample of DOM scripting in FBJS <br/>
</div>
<script>
    var text = document.createElement("input");
    text.setType("text");
    text.setValue("This is a dynamic textbox");
    text.setStyle({padding:"5px", width: "250px",marginTop:"10px" ,
border:"1px solid #bbb"})
    var container = document.getElementById("container");

    container.appendChild(text);
</script>
```

```
Sample of DOM scripting in FBJS

This is a dynamic textbox
```

Let's have a look at the following application, which parses any podcast feed and displays them in a structured format so that you can play it in Facebook. To parse podcast feeds, we have used SimplePie library for PHP. Besides regular features, we will also add some effects in our application using FBJS. Let's get our hands dirty!

```php
<?
//index.php
require_once 'facebook.php'; //from the facebook developers library
$appapikey = 'api key';
$appsecret = 'secret key';
$facebook = new Facebook($appapikey, $appsecret);
$user_id = $facebook->require_login();

include_once("simplepie.inc.php");
$feedurl = urldecode($_POST['url']);
if (empty($feedurl)) $feedurl = "http://www.rockmymonkey.com/webcast/
webcast.xml";
$feed = new SimplePie($feedurl);
$feed->set_raw_data($feeddata);
$feed->handle_content_type();
$feedtitle = $feed->get_title();
echo "<div style='padding:20px;'>";

echo "<h1 style='margin-bottom:20px;'>".$feedtitle. "</h2>";
?>
<form method="POST" action="http://apps.facebook.com/podcastfun/index.
php" style="margin-bottom:20px;" >
Add Feed Url : <input type="text" name="url" />
<input type="submit" value="Load Podcast" value="<?=$feedurl;?>" />
</form>
<?
foreach ($feed->get_items() as $item)
{
    $feedid = md5($item->get_title());
    echo "<div  style='margin-bottom:10px;'>";
    echo "<h2 style='cursor:pointer' clicktotoggle='{$feedid}id'>".$ite
m->get_title()."</h2>";
    echo "<div style='display:none' id='{$feedid}id'><a style='cursor:
pointer' onClick='playPodcast(f{$feedid})'>Play Podcast</a><br/>";
    //echo "<div id='{$feedid}content' >\n";
```

```
        //echo substr($item->get_content(),0,1000);
        echo $item->get_content();
        $enclosure = $item->get_enclosure();
        $link = $enclosure->get_link();
        $title = $enclosure->get_title();
        if (empty($title))
        $title = $item->get_title();
        $artist="";
        echo "<fb:js-string var='f{$feedid}' >";
        echo "<h3>Now Playing {$title} </h3><br/>";
        echo "<fb:mp3 src='{$link}' title='{$title}' artist ='{$artist}'
/><br/><br/>";
        echo $item->get_content();
        echo "</fb:js-string>";
    echo "</div>";
    echo "</div>";
}
echo "</div>";

?>
<script>
function playPodcast(feed)
{
    new Dialog().showMessage("Podcast",feed,"Close");
    return false;
}
</script>
```

Now if you point your browser to this application hosted URL
`http://apps.facebook.com/podcastfun/index.php`, you will see the
following page: (if you are not logged in, you have to log-in first)

Now if you click on any of these titles, you will get something like the following that will display the information about that specific podcast feed:

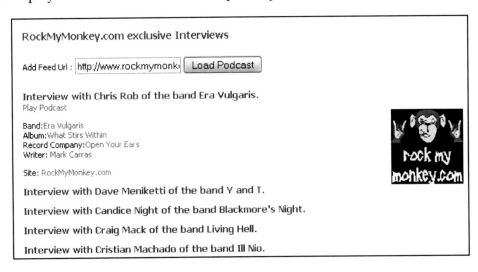

Now you can play the podcast by clicking the **Play Podcast** link just below the title. It will pop up the podcast player in a new dialog box.

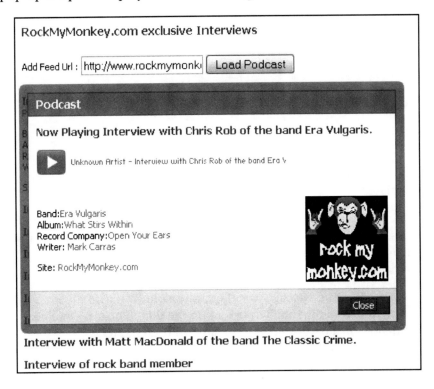

There is a nifty FBJS component called Dialog used in this example. In the later sections, we will learn about it in more detail. But now, let's have a detailed look at the code and some of its confusing parts.

What is used to parse the RSS feeds? This might be your first question at this point. And how did I parse the enclosure (Media Files from RSS) details? Well, I used SimplePie (http://simplepie.org), a very good RSS parser library for PHP developers, and I skipped all the headaches using that.

So what does the following code mean?

```
echo "<fb:js-string var='f{$feedid}' >";
echo "<h3>Now Playing {$title} </h3><br/>";
echo "<fb:mp3 src='{$link}' title='{$title}' artist ='{$artist}'
/><br/><br/>";
echo $item->get_content();
echo "</fb:js-string>";
```

This is something tricky. When you need to display some HTML (or rather, FBML content) in dialog box, you must pass them as pre-rendered FBML to **Dialog** object. `<fb:js-string var='var name'>` is an FBML tag to store the enclosed content inside a JavaScript variable specified in the `var` argument. The name you pass to `var` must be a fully qualified name for a JavaScript variable. Let's take a look at the following FBML Block:

```
<fb:js-string var= 'profile'>
    <fb:name uid= '503274632' useyou= 'false'/>
</fb:js-string>
```

The above will be equivalent to the following FBJS code:

```
var profile = "<a href= 'http://www.facebook.com/profile.
php?id=503274632' >Hasin Hayder</a>"
```

So `<fb:js-string>` is actually used to store pre-rendered FBML content into a JavaScript variable.

So in our code, using `<fb:js-string>` we actually store the pre-rendered FBML content to pass to our dialog box. This variable also contains the code of the podcast player, which we actually render using the `<fb:mp3>` FBML tag. In Chapter 9, we will learn in detail about serving multimedia contents in Facebook.

Now, what happens when we click the **play podcast** link? It actually invokes the `playPodcast()` function that finally pops up in the dialog box. We will learn in detail about dialogs in a dedicated section, later in this chapter.

DRY Means Don't Repeat Yourself

Sometimes in our applications, we need to show and hide a portion of our page right after clicking on something. The point is that we need to change the visibility of some objects on click event. Do you know how we usually code this behavior? The following code block shows us how to do it in JavaScript:

```
<script>
function show(objectid)
{
    document.getElementById(objectid).style.display = "block";
}
function hide(objectid)
{
    document.getElementById(objectid).style.display = "none";
}
function hide(objectid)
{
    var obj = document.getElementById(objectid);
    if (obj.style.display == "none")
    obj.style.display = "block";
    else
    obj.style.display = "none";
}
</script>
```

But in FBJS, this code will be different because FBJS manipulates the stylesheet in a different way:

```
<script>
function show(objectid)
{
    document.getElementById(objectid).setStyle("display", "block");;
}
function hide(objectid)
{
    document.getElementById(objectid).setStyle("display", "none");
}
function hide(objectid)
{
    var obj = document.getElementById(objectid);
    if (obj.getStyle("display")=="none")
    obj.setStyle("display", "block");
    else
    obj.setStyle("display", "none");
}
</script>
```

But the fun is that we don't need to do it at all. You can use the `clicktoshow,,click` `tohide`, and `clicktotoggle` attributes with any button, or link, or any HTML tag, to let FBJS handle this behaviour. Let's have a look at the following section:

```
<div id= 'visible'>
This is Visible
</div>
<div id = "hidden" style= "display:none">
This is Hidden
</div>
<a href= '' clicktoshow= 'visible'>Click to make something visible</
a><br/>
<a href= '' clicktohide= 'hidden'>Click to make something hidden</
a><br/>
<a href= '' clicktotoggle= 'visible'>Click to Toggle</a>
```

Well, of course, it is good if FBJS can handle the pain for us.

Managing Stylesheet with FBJS

As we have already mentioned in the previous section, FBJS manipulates stylesheet in a different way as compared with the usual JavaScript. In pure JavaScript, you can handle stylesheet by accessing them as a property of style object. In FBJS, you have to modify them using the `setStyle` accessor method.

You can change a single property such as this:

```
obj.setStyle('property name', 'property value');
```

And you can modify multiple properties at a time, using curly brackets:

```
obj.setStyle({color: 'black', background: 'white'});
```

But you need to know what the JavaScript equivalent name of each CSS property is. Let's have a look at the section below.

CSS Property	JavaScript Reference
background	background
background-attachment	backgroundAttachment
background-color	backgroundColor
background-image	backgroundImage
background-position	backgroundPosition
background-repeat	backgroundRepeat
Border	border
border-bottom	borderBottom

CSS Property	JavaScript Reference
border-bottom-color	borderBottomColor
border-bottom-style	borderBottomStyle
border-bottom-width	borderBottomWidth
border-color	borderColor
border-left	borderLeft
border-left-color	borderLeftColor
border-left-style	borderLeftStyle
border-left-width	borderLeftWidth
border-right	borderRight
border-right-color	borderRightColor
border-right-style	borderRightStyle
border-right-width	borderRightWidth
border-style	borderStyle
border-top	borderTop
border-top-color	borderTopColor
border-top-style	borderTopStyle
border-top-width	borderTopWidth
border-width	borderWidth
Clear	clear
Clip	clip
Color	color
Cursor	cursor
Display	display
Filter	filter
Font	font
font-family	fontFamily
font-size	fontSize
font-variant	fontVariant
font-weight	fontWeight
Height	height
Left	left
letter-spacing	letterSpacing
line-height	lineHeight
list-style	listStyle
list-style-image	listStyleImage
list-style-position	listStylePosition
list-style-type	listStyleType

CSS Property	JavaScript Reference
Margin	margin
margin-bottom	marginBottom
margin-left	marginLeft
margin-right	marginRight
margin-top	marginTop
Overflow	overflow
Padding	padding
padding-bottom	paddingBottom
padding-left	paddingLeft
padding-right	paddingRight
padding-top	paddingTop
page-break-after	pageBreakAfter
page-break-before	pageBreakBefore
Position	position
Float	styleFloat
text-align	textAlign
text-decoration	textDecoration
text-decoration: blink	textDecorationBlink
text-decoration: line-through	textDecorationLineThrough
text-decoration: none	textDecorationNone
text-decoration: overline	textDecorationOverline
text-decoration: underline	textDecorationUnderline
text-indent	textIndent
text-transform	textTransform
Top	top
vertical-align	verticalAlign
Visibility	visibility
Width	width
z-index	zIndex

Besides that, you can also set CSS class names to an object via FBJS. You can use the `addClassName()` and `removeClassName()` methods as in the following code block:

```
<style>
.visible
{
    display:block;
}
</style>
Document.getElementById('someObject').addClassName("visible");
```

Creating a Drop-Down Menu in FBJS

One of the most challenging jobs in Facebook application development is creating a drop-down menu. In this section, we will learn how to make this drop-down menu.

Here comes the markup. We will decorate it using our FBJS later, to show it like a drop-down menu.

```
<div style="padding:20px">
   <div class="nav" >
      <ul>
         <li style="width:70px;" id="home" >
            <div><a onclick='displayMenu("homechild")' href='#'>Home
                                                 </a></div>
         </li>
         <li  style="width:110px;" >
            <div><a onclick='displayMenu("abchild")'
href='#'>Addressbook</a></div>
            <ul id="abchild" style="background-color:blue">
               <li><a href="#">Videos</a></li>
               <li><a href="#">Screenshots</a></li>
               <li><a href="#">Articles</a></li>
            </ul>
         </li>
         <li  style="width:110px;" >
            <div><a onclick='displayMenu("helpchild")' href='#'>Help
                                                 </a></div>
            <ul id="helpchild" style="background-color:blue" >
               <li><a href="#">Topics</a></li>
               <li><a href="#">Contact us</a></li>
            </ul>
         </li>
      </ul>
   </div>
   <div style="margin-top:140px" ></div>
</div>
```

And this is the stylesheet to make them display properly:

```
<style>
.nav ul
{
   width: 100%;
   list-style: none;
   line-height: 1;
   height:60px;
```

```
        font-weight: bold;
        padding: 0px;
        border-width: 1px 1px;
        margin: 0 0 0 0;
    }
    .nav li {
        float: left;
        padding: 0px;
        padding-top:25px;
        margin-bottom:10px;
    }
    .nav li ul
    {
        display:none;
        padding:5px;
        padding-left:0px;
         background-color:transparent;
        margin-top:10px;
        position: absolute;
        height: auto;
        width: 100px;
        font-weight: normal;
        border-width: 0.25em;
        margin: 0px;
    }

    .nav li ul li{
        float:none;
        padding-top: 5px;
        padding-bottom:5px;
        padding-left:15px;
        color:white;

    }
    .nav a:hover{
        text-decoration:underline;
    }
    .nav li ul li a
    {
        color:white;
        text-decoration:none;
    }
    </style>
```

And finally, here is the tricky part of the code, the FBJS code. I call it tricky in the sense that you could do it just using CSS or Plain JS in regular web pages, and there are thousands of examples available on the Internet. But to do it in FBJS, you have to take care of some more things manually.

```
<script>
    function displayMenu(ch)
    {
    document.getElementById("abchild").setStyle('display','none');

    document.getElementById("helpchild").setStyle('display','none');

        try{
            document.getElementById(ch).setStyle('display','block');
        }
         catch(e){}
    }
</script>
```

The output will look like the following:

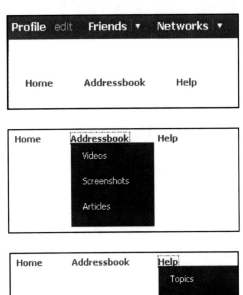

You can extend this example to meet your requirements.

Dialog

To interact with users, FBJS provides you with a nice object named Dialog. Using this object, you can display messages to users as well as take inputs from them. In this section, we will learn how to use dialogs in FBJS.

You can create a Dialog object using the following code:

```
Var dialog = new Dialog();
```

Displaying Information

Using the showMessage() method of a Dialog, you can display any information to your users. This method accepts three parameters.

```
<script>
new Dialog().showMessage("Greeting","Hello, Good Morning","Okay");
</script>
```

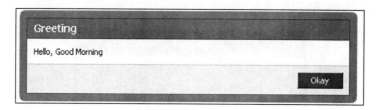

Accepting User Input

If you need only a 'yes' or 'no' answer from your users for any question, you can use the showChoice() method of the Dialog object. It takes four parameters. You can invoke this method as shown below:

```
dialog.showChoice('Title', 'Info' ,'Capton of Ok button','Caption of
Cancel button');
```

And this is how you can manage the user input, after they click **Okay** or **Cancel**:

```
dialog.onconfirm = function(){new Dialog().showMessage("Info","you
clicked 'ok'")};
dialog.oncancel = function(){new Dialog().showMessage("Info","you
clicked 'cancel'")};
```

So, the script will look like this:

```
<script>
var dialog = new Dialog();
dialog.showChoice("Options","Choose Ok Or Cancel","Okay","Cancel");
dialog.onconfirm = function(){new Dialog().showMessage("Info","you
clicked 'ok'")};
dialog.oncancel = function(){new Dialog().showMessage("Info","you
clicked 'cancel'")};
</script>
```

This will output the following dialog box:

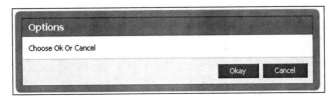

And as soon you click **Okay** or **Cancel**, you will see another dialog box confirming your input.

Contextual or Pop Up?

Using FBJS, you can display two types of dialog box, one is popup, and the other is contextual. The dialog box that you have seen in the examples above, are typical examples of pop up. Let's have a look at the following code to see what a contextual dialog is:

```
<div style="padding:20px">
<a id="link" style='cursor:pointer'  onclick="showDialog(this);">Click
me to see a contextual dialog</a>
</div>
<script>
function showDialog(linker){
    //context = document.getElementById("link");
    new Dialog(Dialog.DIALOG_CONTEXTUAL).setContext(linker).showMessage
("Greeting","Hello, Good Morning","Okay");
}
</script>
```

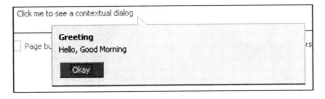

Please note that you must call `setContext()` before calling `showMessage()` or `showChoice()`. If you call it later, the dialog will never be shown in the right place but in top left corner of the page.

Advanced Input System Using Dialogs

If you are thinking that there is just one way to get input from users such as **Okay** or **Cancel**, you are wrong! You can take whatever input you want from your users. You can pass any valid pre-rendered FBML block to dialogs. Using that facility, you can design your dialogs as you wish. Let's have a look at the following example by which you can take written inputs from your users.

```
<div style="padding:20px">
<a id="link" href="#" onclick="showDialog(this);">Click me to see a
contextual dialog</a>
</div>
<fb:js-string var='inputs'>
    How are you feeling now? <br/>
    <input type="text" id="userinput" />
</fb:js-string>
<script>

function showDialog(linker){
    //context = document.getElementById("link");
    new Dialog(Dialog.DIALOG_CONTEXTUAL).setContext(linker).showMessage
("Greeting",inputs,"Okay").onconfirm=function(){
        data = "So you are feeling " + document.getElementById("userinpu
t").getValue() +"?  thats cool!";
        new Dialog().showMessage("Info",data,"Okay");
        return false;
    };
}
</script>
```

This will create the following dialog box when executed. Click on the link, and type whatever you want:

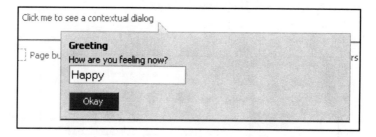

Now click on **Okay** and you will get the following response:

Now it's up to you to how wild you want to get in designing these input dialogs.

Events

Another important part of FBJS is events. If you are familiar with event management in JavaScript, then managing events will not be a big deal for you in FBJS. Almost everything is the same. You have to use the addEventListener () function to attach listeners to an event.

The addEventListener () function takes two arguments. The first one is the name of the event to listen, and the second one is the callback. Let's have a look at the following code to understand how to attach an event.

```
<div style="padding:20px">
    <div id="somediv">
        Some Content
    </div>
    <input type="button" id="somebutton" value="Click Me" />
</div>
<script>
    button = document.getElementById("somebutton");
    button.addEventListener("click",hide);

    function hide(event)
    {
        document.getElementById("somediv").setStyle("display","none");
    }
</script>
```

You can find out who fired the event easily, using the `event.target.getId()` method of an event object. Take a look at the above code. As soon as you click the button, you will see the following dialog box:

```
function hide(event)
{
    document.getElementById("somediv").setStyle("display","none");
    firedby = event.target.getId();
    new Dialog().showMessage("Info","This event was fired by
"+firedby+"","Okay")
}
```

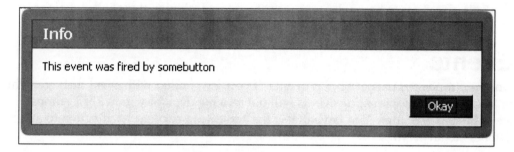

Here `somebutton` is the ID of the button that fired the event.

This method is certainly useful due to a specific bug in FBJS. When you attach an event to a DOM node, the event has been automatically added to all the child nodes in that node. This might not be an expected behaviour. So you can check which object is invoking the event listener, and then take action using `getId()`.

There are some other useful methods available to this event object, which you will need, in order to develop sophisticated event-based applications. Lets have a look at those methods:

- `stopPropagation()` — This method stops the propagation of an event further to any DOM node. Otherwise, when an event occurs in a child object, the on[event] fires for both child and parent containing that.

- `cancelDefault()` — Cancels the default behaviour of the event. To understand it, take a look at the following code block:

```
<div style="padding:20px">
    <textarea id="sometextarea">
    </textarea>
</div>
<script>
    ta = document.getElementById("sometextarea");
```

```
ta.addEventListener("keydown",keydown);
function keydown(ev)
{
    keycode = ev.keyCode;
    if (keycode==83)
     ev.preventDefault();
    //new Dialog().showMessage("Info","you have pressed
"+keycode+"","Okay")
}
</script>
```

As soon you press any key in the text area, if it is *s*, it will never be displayed, as we cancel the event when the keycode is 83 (that means *s*).

- `listEventListeners(eventName)` — Returns an array of handles of all the events that have been added to this event. Events that were added in FBML using the `<event>` attributes will also be included.

- `purgeEventListeners(eventName)` — Removes all event listeners for a given event. This also removes events that were added as attributes in FBML.

AJAX

AJAX stands for Asynchronous JavaScript and XML. This technology is used to seamlessly process data behind the scenes using an object called `XmlHttpRequest`. We are not going to discuss details of core AJAX in this section, but how can you use this technology in Facebook applications using FBJS. Let's have a look at the following code, which places an AJAX call, and tells you the current time in GMT. This is not actually possible using JavaScript or FBJS. This example is so nice that it is taken directly from Facebook wiki:

```
These links demonstrate the Ajax object:<br />
<a href="#" onclick="do_ajax(Ajax.JSON); return false;">JSON</a><br />
<a href="#" onclick="do_ajax(Ajax.RAW); return false;">RAW</a><br />
<a href="#" onclick="do_ajax(Ajax.FBML); return false;">FBML</a><br />
<label><input type="checkbox" id="requirelogin" checked="checked"
/><span>Require Login?</span></label><br />
<div><span id="ajax1"></span><span id="ajax2"></span></div>

<script><!--
function do_ajax(type) {
  var ajax = new Ajax();
  ajax.responseType = type;
  switch (type) {
    case Ajax.JSON:
```

```
        ajax.ondone = function(data) {
          document.getElementById('ajax1').setTextValue(data.message + '
The current time is: ' +  data.time + '. ');
          document.getElementById('ajax2').setInnerFBML(data.fbml_test);
        }
        break;
      case Ajax.FBML:
        ajax.ondone = function(data) {
          document.getElementById('ajax1').setInnerFBML(data);
          document.getElementById('ajax2').setTextValue('');
        }
        break;
      case Ajax.RAW:
        ajax.ondone = function(data) {
          document.getElementById('ajax1').setTextValue(data);
          document.getElementById('ajax2').setTextValue('');
        }
        break;
    }
    ajax.requireLogin = document.getElementById('requirelogin').
getChecked();
    ajax.post(' http://javapark.net/hasin/fb/rssdemo/gmttime.
php?t='+type);
  }
//--></script>
```

This code posts AJAX call, based on the user input, either in JSON, XML or RAW format. If the call is successful, then it replaces the value of the textbox with the response data. If the `requirelogin` is checked, user would have to log in to this application using their Facebook credentials.

And this is the PHP code of `gmttime.php`:

```
<?php
$user = isset($_POST['fb_sig_user']) ? $_POST['fb_sig_user'] : null;
if ($_GET['t'] == 0) { // Ajax.RAW
  echo 'This is a raw string. The current time is: '.date('r').', and
you are '.($user ? 'uid: #'.$user : 'anonymous').'.';
} else if ($_GET['t'] == 1) { // Ajax.JSON
  echo '{"message": "This is a JSON object.", "time": "'.date('r').'"',
"fbml_test": "Hello, '.($user ? '<fb:name uid='.$user.' useyou=false
/>' : 'anonymous').'."}';
} else if ($_GET['t'] == 2) { // Ajax.FBML
  echo 'This is an FBML string. The current time is: '.date('r').',
and you are '.($user ? '<fb:name uid='.$user.' useyou=false />' :
'anonymous').'.';
}
?>
```

The output is as follows:

These links demonstrate the Ajax object:
JSON
RAW
FBML
☑ Require Login?

And when you click any of these links, you will get an output like this:

These links demonstrate the Ajax object:
JSON
RAW
FBML
☑ Require Login?
This is a JSON object. The current time is: Mon, 10 Dec 2007 01:38:44 -0700. Hello, Hasin Hayder.

Common Tasks

While working with AJAX in FBML, some questions might pop into your mind. Here are some of the most likely questions:

Posting Parameters to Server Side Code

You can do this with the help of the second argument of the `Ajax.post()` method. Please remember that there is a limitation to sending JSON data to server via AJAX call. The parameter string can be no more than 5000 chars.

```
var params = { "param1" : value1, "param2" : value2 };
ajax.post("url", queryParams);
```

If you look carefully, you will find that it is actually a JSON encoded string containing the name and value of all the parameters to post. If you find it difficult to write such strings manually, you can use the `json_encode()` function to do it for you, and that is also recommended by Facebook. Have a look at the following sample code:

```
<?php
    $data = array("param1"=> "value1", "param2" => "value2");
    jsondata = json_encode($data);
    echo $jsondata;
?>
```

This will output the following data:

```
{"param1":"value1","param2":"value2"}
```

Posting Multibyte Characters

If you are working with a language other than English, then you must be familiar with multibyte strings, which are also known as Unicode text. In the following example, we will see how to pass multibyte strings to server side script via AJAX calls:

```
<div style="padding:20px">
Send this text to server side
<input type="text" id="multibyte" />
<input type="button" value="Send" onclick="send()" />
<br/><br/>

<div id="returnedtext"></div>
</div>
<script>
function send(type) {
   var ajax = new Ajax();
   ajax.responseType = Ajax.RAW;

   ajax.ondone = function(data) {
       document.getElementById('returnedtext').setTextValue(data);
   }
   data = document.getElementById('multibyte').getValue();
   var params = {"data":data};
   ajax.post('http://javapark.net/hasin/fb/rssdemo/unicode.
php',params);
}
</script>
```

And the server side code that just displays the input data is here. If the encoding is preserved, you should see the same as your input after submitting the form.

```
<?
header("Content-type: text/html charset='utf-8' ");
$data = $_POST['data'];
echo "You submitted {$data}";
?>
```

The output will look like this.

Canceling an AJAX Request

Just use the `Ajax.abort()` method to cancel any AJAX request. This is particularly useful when designing projects such as auto-complete text boxes. While designing such a widget, we place AJAX call after every key stroke, to find the matching words. So as soon as a new key is pressed, you can cancel the previous AJAX call from being transmitted. And that will keep the latest AJAX call always live, dismissing the previous calls. So just before placing a new AJAX request, call `Ajax.abort()` to dismiss the previous AJAX call.

Making Sure that Users have to Log In for the AJAX Request

Use the `requireLogin` parameter, and set it as `true`. If you set this to true, the AJAX call will require the user to be logged into your application before it can go through. The AJAX call will be made at that time with the regular `fb_sig` parameters containing the user's identity. If they refuse to log in, the AJAX call will fail.

Summary

In this chapter, we learned how to use FBJS in our Facebook application effectively, and how it can boost usability and ease the development process. FBJS is one of the most vital parts of every Facebook application. So you have to try coding in FBJS to learn to write it effectively.

In the next chapter, we will learn about Notifications, which is another important part of making your application popular; and also a way to interact with users. Till then, happy coding in FBJS!

6
Feeds

Feeds are a very important part of Facebook Applications. They are used to publish notifications and news in a user's profile. So, feeds are the best way to keep the friends of the users up-to-date about the user's current activities. Feeds are also a great way to publicize your applications, if you know what I mean.

In this chapter, we will go into the details of managing feeds (both news feed and mini feed) using Facebook REST APIs. The following sections will help you understand what the major differences between these two types of feed are, and how to use them properly in your application.

What Are Feeds?

Feeds are the way to publish news in Facebook. As we have already mentioned before, there are two types of feeds in Facebook, News feed and Mini feed. News feed instantly tracks activities of a user's online friends, ranging from changes in relationship status to added photos to wall comments. Mini feed appears on individuals' profiles and highlights recent social activity. You can see your news feed right after you log in, and point your browser to `http://www.facebook.com/home. php`. It looks like the following, which is, in fact, my news feed.

Mini feeds are seen in your profile page, displaying your recent activities and look like the following one:

Only the last 10 entries are being displayed in the mini feed section of the profile page. But you can always see the complete list of mini feeds by going to `http://www.facebook.com/minifeed.php`. Also the mini feed of any user can be accessed from `http://www.facebook.com/minifeed.php?id=userid`.

There is another close relation between news feed and mini feed. When applications publish a mini feed in your profile, it will also appear in your friend's news feed page.

How to Publish Feeds

Facebook provides three APIs to publish mini feeds and news feeds. But these are restricted to call not more than 10 times for a particular user in a 48 hour cycle. This means you can publish a maximum of 10 feeds in a specific user's profile within 48 hours. The following three APIs help to publish feeds:

- `feed_publishStoryToUser`—This function publishes the story to the news feed of any user (limited to call once every 12 hours).

- `feed_publishActionOfUser`—This one publishes the story to a user's mini feed, and to his or her friend's news feed (limited to call 10 times in a rolling 48 hour slot).

- `feed_publishTemplatizedAction`—This one also publishes mini feeds and news feeds, but in an easier way (limited to call 10 times in a rolling 48 hour slot).

You can test this API also from `http://developers.facebook.com/tools.php?api`, and by choosing **Feed Preview Console**, which will give you the following interface:

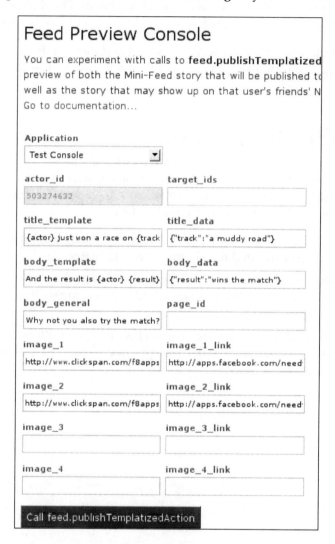

And once you execute the sample, like the previous one, it will preview the sample of your feed.

Sample Application to Play with Feeds

Let's publish some news to our profile, and test how the functions actually work. In this section, we will develop a small application (RateBuddies) by which we will be able to send messages to our friends, and then publish our activities as a mini feed. The purpose of this application is to display friends list and rate them in different categories (Awesome, All Square, Loser, etc.).

Here is the code of our application:

index.php

```php
<?
include_once("prepend.php"); //the Lib and key container
?>
<div style="padding:20px;">
<?
if (!empty($_POST['friend_sel']))
{
    $friend = $_POST['friend_sel'];
    $rating = $_POST['rate'];

    $title = "<fb:name uid='{$fbuser}' useyou='false' /> just  <a
href='http://apps.facebook.com/ratebuddies/'>Rated</a> <fb:name
uid='{$friend}' useyou='false' /> as a  '{$rating}' ";
    $body = "Why not you also <a href='http://apps.facebook.com/
ratebuddies/'>rate your friends</a>?";

try{
//now publish the story to user's mini feed and on his friend's news
feed
    $facebook->api_client->feed_publishActionOfUser($title, $body,
    null, $null,null, null, null, null, null, null, 1);
    } catch(Exception $e) {
        //echo "Error when publishing feeds: "; echo $e->getMessage();
    }
}
?>
    <h1>Welcome to RateBuddies, your gateway to rate your friends</h1>

    <div style="padding-top:10px;">
        <form method="POST">
            Seect a friend: <br/><br/>
            <fb:friend-selector uid="<?=$fbuser;?>" name="friendid"
idname="friend_sel" />
            <br/><br/><br/>

            And your friend is: <br/>
            <table>
```

```
        <tr>
            <td valign="middle"><input name="rate" type="radio"
value="funny" /></td>
            <td valign="middle">Funny</td>
        </tr>
        <tr>
            <td valign="middle"><input name="rate" type="radio"
value="hot tempered" /></td>
            <td valign="middle">Hot Tempered</td>
        </tr>
        <tr>
            <td valign="middle"><input name="rate" type="radio"
value="awesome" /></td>
            <td valign="middle">Awesome</td>
        </tr>

        <tr>
            <td valign="middle"><input name="rate" type="radio"
value="naughty professor" /></td>
            <td valign="middle">Naughty Professor</td>
        </tr>
        <tr>
            <td valign="middle"><input name="rate" type="radio"
value="looser" /></td>
                <td valign="middle">Looser</td>
        </tr>
        <tr>
            <td valign="middle"><input name="rate" type="radio"
value="empty veseel" /></td>
            <td valign="middle">Empty Vessel</td>
        </tr>
        <tr>
            <td valign="middle"><input name="rate" type="radio"
value="foxy" /></td>
            <td valign="middle">Foxy</td>
        </tr>
        <tr>
            <td valign="middle"><input name="rate" type="radio"
value="childish" /></td>
            <td valign="middle">Childish</td>
        </tr>
    </table>
      <input type="submit" value="Rate Buddy"/>
  </form>
 </div>
</div>
```

`index.php` includes another file called `prepend.php`. In that file, we initialized the `facebook api` client using the API key and Secret key of the current application. It is a good practice to keep them in separate file because we need to use them throughout our application, in as many pages as we have. Here is the code of that file:

prepend.php

```php
<?php
// this defines some of your basic setup
include 'client/facebook.php'; // the facebook API library

// Get these from http://www.facebook.com/developers/apps.php
http://www.facebook.com/developers/apps.php$api_key = 'your api
key';//the api ket of this application
$secret  = 'your secret key'; //the secret key

$facebook = new Facebook($api_key, $secret);

    //catch the exception that gets thrown if the cookie has an invalid
session_key in it
    try {
      if (!$facebook->api_client->users_isAppAdded()) {
        $facebook->redirect($facebook->get_add_url());
      }
    } catch (Exception $ex) {
      //this will clear cookies for your application and redirect them
to a login prompt
      $facebook->set_user(null, null);
      $facebook->redirect($appcallbackurl);
    }

?>
```

The client is a standard Facebook REST API client, which is available directly from Facebook.

If you are not sure about these API keys, then point your browser to `http://www.facebook.com/developers/apps.php` and collect the API key and secret key from there. Here is a screenshot of that page:

Just collect your API key and Secret Key from this page, when you develop your own application.

Now, when you point your browser to `http://apps.facebooks.com/ratebuddies` and successfully add that application, it will look like this:

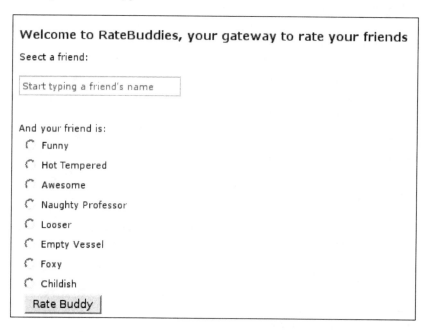

To see how this app works, type a friend in the box, **Select a friend**, and click on any rating such as **Funny** or **Foxy**. Then click on the **Rate Buddy** button. As soon as the page submits, open your profile page and you will see that it has published a mini feed in your profile.

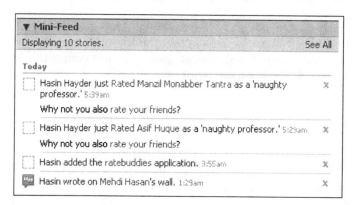

So How Did it Work?

We have used the following code for the friend selector. It takes three parameters. The uid is the currently logged in user's id whose friend list will be rendered. For choosing friends, the second one is **name**, which will act as the POST field name when the user submits it. This field will contain the name of the chosen friend. The third parameter is the POST field name that will hold the chosen friend's id.

```
<fb:friend-selector uid="<?=$fbuser;?>" name="friendid"
idname="friend_sel" />
```

So after submitting, you will get the friend's id and name as $_POST['friend_sel'] and $_POST['friendid'].

Now take a look at the following PHP code that publishes the mini feed:

```
<?
if (!empty($_POST['friend_sel']))
{
    $friend = $_POST['friend_sel'];
    $rating = $_POST['rate'];

    $title = "<fb:name uid='{$fbuser}' useyou='false' /> just  <a
href='http://apps.facebook.com/ratebuddies/'>Rated</a> <fb:name
uid='{$friend}' useyou='false' /> as a  '{$rating}' ";
    $body = "Why not you also <a href='http://apps.facebook.com/
ratebuddies/'>rate your friends</a>?";
    try{
        $facebook->api_client->feed_publishActionOfUser($title, $body,
        null, $null,null, null, null, null, null, 1);
    } catch(Exception $e) {
        echo "Error when publishing feeds: "; echo $e->getMessage();
    }
}
?>
```

It uses the FBML tags to render the user's name and uses
feed_publishActionOfUser() API to publish the news feed.

 Please note that you can only use <fb:name/>, <fb:link/>, <a>, <b>, and <i> tag in mini feed's body. And in title, you can only use <fb:name/>, <fb:link/>, and <a> tag. If you use any other tag, they will be stripped by Facebook along with the enclosed content.

There is no guarantee that the mini feed will also be published in your friend's news feed. It may or may not be published based on their news feed settings and the competing stories.

Publishing News Feed

Let's add more functionality to our application. We want to enable news feeds in the personal news feed section, which will tell you how many of your friends have been rated in the last 12 hours. If there is any, you will be able to see them in your news feed.

For this, we need to use a database with our application, which will contain the time of rating and the ids of both the users who rate, and the users who are rated. We will also store the given rating. Let's do it. Here is our table schema.

Table Rates

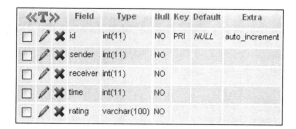

«T»			Field	Type	Null	Key	Default	Extra
☐	✏	✖	id	int(11)	NO	PRI	*NULL*	auto_increment
☐	✏	✖	sender	int(11)	NO			
☐	✏	✖	receiver	int(11)	NO			
☐	✏	✖	time	int(11)	NO			
☐	✏	✖	rating	varchar(100)	NO			

Now let's take a look at the revised code of our `index.php`:

```php
<?
include_once("prepend.php");
mysql_pconnect($dbhost, $dbuser, $dbpwd);
mysql_select_db($dbname);
?>
<div style="padding:20px;">
<?
if (!empty($_POST['friend_sel']))
{
    $time = time();
    $friend = $_POST['friend_sel'];
    $rating = $_POST['rate'];
    mysql_query("INSERT INTO rates (id, sender, receiver,rating,
`time`) VALUES (null,{$fbuser},{$friend},'{$rating}',{$time})");

    $title = "<fb:name uid='{$fbuser}' useyou='false' /> just  <a
href='http://apps.facebook.com/ratebuddies/'>Rated</a> <fb:name
uid='{$friend}' useyou='false' /> as {$rating}.";
    $body = "Why not you also <a href='http://apps.facebook.com/
ratebuddies/'>rate your friends</a>?";
    try{
        $facebook->api_client->feed_publishActionOfUser($title, $body,
```

```
                null, $null,null, null, null, null, null, null, 1);
        } catch(Exception $e) {
            echo "Error when publishing feeds: "; echo $e->getMessage();
        }
}

//search for friends who have been rated in last 12 hours where sender
is not you and receiver is any of your friends

$friends = $facebook->api_client->friends_get();
$temp = join(",",$friends);

$checkpoint = time()-12*60*60;
$result = mysql_query("SELECT * FROM rates WHERE `time`>{$checkpoint}
AND sender != {$fbuser} AND receiver IN ($temp)");
if (mysql_num_rows($result)>0)
{
    $info = $facebook->api_client->users_getInfo($friends,array("uid",
"name"));
    $friendsname = array();
    foreach ($info as $_temp)
    {
        $friendsname[$_temp['uid']] = $_temp['name'];
    }
    $report = "";
    while ($data = mysql_fetch_assoc($result))
    {
        $report .= "<a href='http://www.facebook.com/profile.php?id={
$data['sender']}'>{$friendsname[$data['sender']]}</a> just rated <a
href='http://www.facebook.com/profile.php?id={$data['receiver']}'>{$fr
iendsname[$data['receiver']]}</a> as {$data['rating']}. ";
    }

    $newstitle = "Friends recently rated...";
    try{
        $facebook->api_client->feed_publishStoryToUser($newstitle,
$report,
        null, $null,null, null, null, null, null, null, 1);
    } catch(Exception $e) {
        //          echo "Error when publishing feeds: ";
                                            echo $e->getMessage();
    }
}
?>
    <h1>Welcome to RateBuddies, your gateway to rate your friends</h1>

    <div style="padding-top:10px;">
        <form method="POST">
```

```
           Seect a friend: <br/><br/>
           <fb:friend-selector uid="<?=$fbuser;?>" name="friendid"
   idname="friend_sel" />
           <br/><br/><br/>

           And your friend is: <br/>
           <table>
              <tr>
                 <td valign="middle"><input name="rate" type="radio"
   value="funny" /></td>
                 <td valign="middle">Funny</td>
              </tr>
              <tr>
                 <td valign="middle"><input name="rate" type="radio"
   value="hot tempered" /></td>
                 <td valign="middle">Hot Tempered</td>
              </tr>
              <tr>
                 <td valign="middle"><input name="rate" type="radio"
   value="awesome" /></td>
                 <td valign="middle">Awesome</td>
              </tr>
              <tr>
                 <td valign="middle"><input name="rate" type="radio"
   value="all sqaure" /></td>
                 <td valign="middle">All Square</td>
              </tr>
              <tr>
                 <td valign="middle"><input name="rate" type="radio"
   value="naughty professor" /></td>
                 <td valign="middle">Naughty Professor</td>
              </tr>
              <tr>
                 <td valign="middle"><input name="rate" type="radio"
   value="looser" /></td>
                 <td valign="middle">Looser</td>
              </tr>
              <tr>
                 <td valign="middle"><input name="rate" type="radio"
   value="empty veseel" /></td>
                 <td valign="middle">Empty Vessel</td>
              </tr>
              <tr>
                 <td valign="middle"><input name="rate" type="radio"
   value="foxy" /></td>
                 <td valign="middle">Foxy</td>
```

```
            </tr>
            <tr>
                <td valign="middle"><input name="rate" type="radio"
                                            value="childish" /></td>
                <td valign="middle">Childish</td>
            </tr>
        </table>
          <input type="submit" value="Rate Buddy"/>
    </form>
  </div>
</div>
```

So how is it working? Once somebody rates his or her friends, we store the result in our table using the following code:

```
if (!empty($_POST['friend_sel']))
{
    $time = time();
    $friend = $_POST['friend_sel'];
    $rating = $_POST['rate'];
    mysql_query("INSERT INTO rates (id, sender, receiver,rating,
`time`) VALUES (null,{$fbuser},{$friend},'{$rating}',{$time})");
    echo "INSERT INTO rates (id, sender, receiver, `time`) VALUES (null
,{$fbuser},{$friend},{$time})";
    echo mysql_error();
```

Now, comes the tricky part. We need to retrieve all the friends of the currently logged in user who had been rated in the last 12 hours. But we must keep in mind that we will not pick those who are not rated by the logged in user, but someone else. We'll do it using the following code:

```
 $friends = $facebook->api_client->friends_get();
$temp = join(",",$friends);

$checkpoint = time()-12*60*60;
$result = mysql_query("SELECT * FROM rates WHERE `time`>{$checkpoint}
AND sender != {$fbuser} AND receiver IN ($temp)");
```

It will give you friends that you have rated in the last 12 hours.

Here's another tricky part. While publishing the mini feed, we displayed the names of our friends using the `<fb:name>` tag, which is not supported in news feeds. So we must find another way to display their names. We'll fetch all the friend's names using `users_getInfo()` API and store them in a temporary array. Later, we'll use that array to display the names. Finally, we'll publish the news feed. Look at the following code:

```
if (mysql_num_rows($result)>0)
{
    $info = $facebook->api_client->users_getInfo($friends,array
                                                ("uid","name"));
    $friendsname = array();
    foreach ($info as $_temp)
    {
        $friendsname[$_temp['uid']] = $_temp['name'];
    }
    $report = "";
    while ($data = mysql_fetch_assoc($result))
    {
        $report .= "<a href='http://www.facebook.com/profile.php?id={
$data['sender']}'>{$friendsname[$data['sender']]}</a> just rated <a
href='http://www.facebook.com/profile.php?id={$data['receiver']}'>{$fr
iendsname[$data['receiver']]}</a> as {$data['rating']}. ";
    }

    $newstitle = "Friends recently rated...";
    try{
        $facebook->api_client->feed_publishStoryToUser($newstitle,
$report,
        null, $null,null, null, null, null, null, 1);
    } catch(Exception $e) {
        //          echo "Error when publishing feeds: "; echo $e-
>getMessage();
    }
}
```

So how would the output look like? You are definitely thinking about it, right? Have a look:

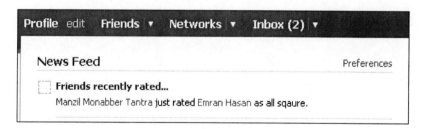

Difference between These Two Methods

There are significant differences between `feed_publishStoryToUser()` and `feed_publishActionOfUser()` functions. The Facebook Wiki has a comprehensive list of key differences at `http://wiki.developers.facebook.com/index.php/PublishActionOfUser_vs._PublishStoryToUser`, which is worth giving a look.

	publishActionOfUser	publishStoryToUser
Publishes to minifeed	Yes	No
Publishes to newsfeed	Friends' (possibly)	Own
Prefix	The user's name is a prefix to the title (if you don't specify <fb:userlink>)	There is no prefix added to your title
Limits on usage	Limited always	Unlimited to app developer's newsfeed
Send restrictions	10 times per user in any 48 hour period	Once per user every 12 hours
Tags Allowed in Title	fb:userlink, fb:name, a *the 'a' and 'fb:userlink' tags can be used a maximum of once each in the title	a
Tags Allowed in Body	fb:userlink, fb:name, a, b, i	a, b, i

Besides the above, each of these functions has the following restrictions:

- Title length is limited to 60 characters (excluding tags).
- Body length is limited to 200 characters (excluding tags).
- Included images must have an associated link.
- The associated image links must be http links. Notably, https links do not work.

feed_publishTemplatizedAction

This is another API to publish news feed to a friend of the user. It helps developers to be more structured. This function takes a number of parameters, and all the rules of `publisActionOfUser` are affected by the same kind of uncertainty and delay that is encountered while publishing the feed. Spam and server load are the major factors for that.

If you take a look at the definition of this API, you will find the following:

Param	Description
title_template	A template which contains the title of the feed
title_data	A JSON encoded string containing the value of the template variables
body_template	Template containing the text of the body
body_data	A JSON encoded string containing the value of the template variables
body_general	Additional template data to include in the body
image_1	The URL of an image to be displayed in the Feed story
image_1_link	The URL destination after a click on the image referenced by image_1
image_2	The URL of an image to be displayed in the Feed story
image_2_link	The URL destination after a click on the image referenced by image_2
image_3	The URL of an image to be displayed in the Feed story
image_3_link	The URL destination after a click on the image referenced by image_3
image_4	The URL of an image to be displayed in the Feed story
image_4_link	The URL destination after a click on the image referenced by image_4
target_id	Comma-delimited list of IDs of friends of the actor, used for stories about a direct action between the actor and these targets of his/her action. This is required if either the title_template or body_template includes the token {target}.

This API can publish up to four images in the feed. You can also make them clickable by supplying the destination URL along with them. Let's have a look at the following code, which will show you how to use this API. After a specific event in your application, you can use code like the following one:

```php
<?php

$titleTemplate + "{actor} gifts a {item} to {friend}";
$titleData = array("item"=>"flower","friend"=>"<fb:name uid='some
uid'>");

$bodyTemplate = "color of that {item} is {color}";
$bodyData = array("color"=>"red","item"=>"flower");

$image1 = "absolute url of an image";
$image1Target = "target url when clicked over that image";

$facebook->api_client->feed_publishTemplatizedAction($titleTemplate,j
son_encode($titleData),$bodyTemplate,json_encode($bodyData),$image1,$
image1Target);

?>
```

There are some default values, which are replaced by Facebook itself, while publishing the feed. For example the value of `actor` in the above feed will always be replaced as the viewer or currently logged in user. There is a fantastic article on this API and you are encouraged to read it.

```
http://facebook-developer.net/2008/01/21/how-to-successfully-publish-
widespread-news-feed-stories/
```

Summary

News feed and mini feeds are a very important part for delivering news to the users of your applications, and keep their friends up-to-date about the activities. In this chapter, we have learnt how to deal with Feed APIs provided by Facebook. We have also learnt the major difference between these APIs and their usage.

In the next chapter, we will add more features to our application by learning how to send notifications directly to the friends. Notifications and Invitations are a very important part of publicizing your application. Besides that, it will also be fun to invite your friends to use your application. In the next chapter, we will also learn how to design a nice invitation system that will certainly boost up the popularity. Till then, happy feed programming !

7
Invitations and Notifications

If you ever wonder what the secret of viral marketing of Facebook applications is, then you will find that it is all about invitations. Facebook allows an application user to invite his friends to use that application. And, as an application developer, your role is to determine when and how to let them invite their friends. You also have to decide how to make it a sure success so that the friends of your application user will pay a visit to your application. Besides this, Facebook also allows application developers to let their user send email notifications.

In this chapter, we will focus on:

- Creating a successful invitation system
- Creating a successful notification system
- Using notifications efficiently
- Sending email

Invitations

Invitations in Facebook applications are used to send emails to friends of a user of that application. Using this email (and sometimes links in notifications), any one of his or her friends can subscribe to that Facebook application. Invitations are a great way of promoting your application. Before a recent update, users of an application were able to send invitations to all their friends at a time, and Facebook application developers had to redesign the whole system from scratch using Facebook API.

After a recent change in the invitation system, Facebook added some strict policies such as, a user can invite only 20 of his friends each day. Facebook is also providing a nice widget so that you don't have to design everything from scratch.

In this section, we will design an invitation system for our RSS feed application. Let's take a look at a invitation page. The following Facebook application is one where I participated. The URL of this page is

`http://apps.facebook.com/needforspeed/invite.php.`

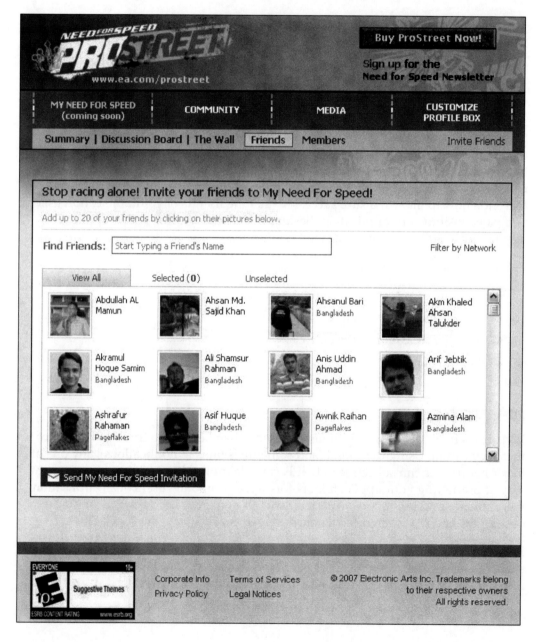

An invitation system on Facebook has different parts. You cannot change the default look and feel of this one unless you are a CSS hacker. But the game begins when you select some of your friends, and click **Send Invitation**.

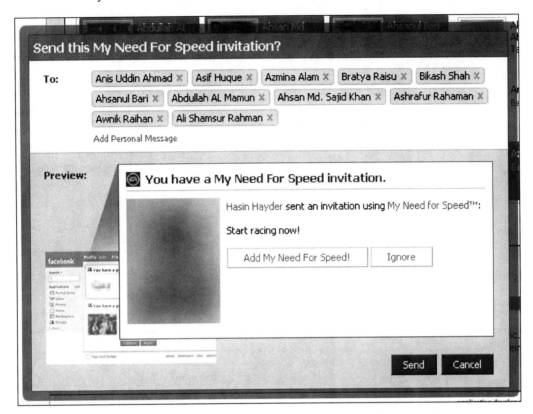

You can still remove some of your selected friends by clicking the **X** besides their names at the top of this dialogue box.

To design such a system, we need to understand some FBML tags:

- `fb:request-form`
- `fb:req-choice`
- `fb:request-form-submit`
- `fb:application-name`
- `fb:multi-friend-input`
- `fb:friend-selector`
- `fb:multi-friend-selector` (condensed)

The primary widget for inviting friends is created using the `fb:request-form` tag. So let's have a look at it first. This is the example of a typical invitation code. It will show a nice invitation to the users of your application.

```
<fb:request-form
    action="invitation processor page"
    method="POST"
    invite="true"
    type="Application Name"
    content="Content of your Mail">
  <fb:multi-friend-selector
      showborder="false"
      actiontext="Invite your friends to the Application Name"
      exclude_ids="exclude friends who are currently using this app"
      max="20" />
</fb:request-form>
```

Let's take a look at the quick-reference of `fb:request-form`.

fb:request-form

This function takes the following parameters:

Parameter	What is it?		
Action	This parameter tells where this page will submit all the information when someone clicks the **send invitation** or **skip** button.		
Method	GET or POST, the way information will be submitted.	What is it?	
Invite	true or false. When set as true, this invitation will go as invitation, otherwise as a request. The change actually reflects the content of the invitation that the user will get.	User id of whose album info you are trying to retrieve.	
Type	This one is usually set the same as the application name. You can set anything that reflects the context or event.	What is it?	

Let's take a look at other tags also.

fb:req-choice

Using this tag, you can insert a button in your request message, and define the name and target URL. So when a user receives your invitation, they will also see the button inside it, and when they click that button, they will be redirected to the URL that you specify. This is certainly useful if you want them to install the application — just by providing a nice button inside your invitation message.

This tag accepts two parameters, as shown below:

Parameter	What is it?
url	This is the target URL used to redirect the user on click.
label	The caption of the button.
	`<fb:req-choice url="http://apps.facebook.com/example/confirm.php" label="Confirm" />`

Don't use "ignore" as the caption of this request button. Ignore button is there by default. So if you insert one more ignore button, chances are that you could lose all the buttons inside.

fb:request-form-submit

This tag will display a submit button inside your invitation form. If you want to display the user's name or the full name inside this button, you can take the help of the two parameters that this tag accepts.

Parameter	What is it?
uid	The user id to which you want to send this invitation.
label	Caption of the button. If you want to show the first name of the user, then use %n or if you want to show the full name, then use %N.
	`<fb:request-form-submit uid= 'some uid' label= 'send %n an Invitation' />`

fb:multi-friend-selector

This one is used to draw a friend selector widget anywhere in the canvas page. That's why we use it in our `fb:request-form` to display that widget. The parameters of this tag are as follows:

Parameter	What is it?
actiontext	Here, you specify what to display at the top of this friend selector as the heading.
showborder	`true` or `false`. Name explains the task.
rows	The number of rows, the friends will be shown in. The default value of this parameter is 5. You can choose anything from 3 to 10.
max	The number of friends a user can select at a time to send an invitation to. Keep it at 20. We'll explain the "why" of this later.
exclude_ids	A comma separated list of friends who are not to be shown in this selector object. You can use this to exclude your friends who have already installed this application.
bypass	This will be the label of the **skip** button.
condensed	`true`. This will create a condensed page (as the name says) that looks far different from a full version.

fb:multi-friend-input

Instead of a multi-friend selector, you can also use a multi-friend input in a `fb:request-form`. But the friend selector is much more user-friendly as compared to a friend input. At run time, it looks like this:

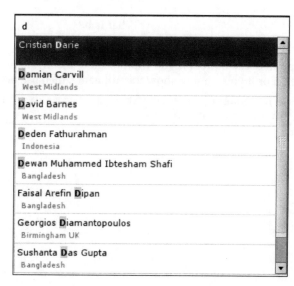

Using multi-input, you can select an arbitrary numbers of friends. The usage of multi-friend selector is simple. Let's have a look at the parameters first:

Parameter	What is it?
width	This is the width of the input box.
border_color	The HTML color code to color the border of this selector panel.
include_me	If this is set to true, you can select yourself. By default, it is set to false.
max	This specifies the maximum number of friends you can select. For sending invitations, you can keep it at 20 (maximum), which is default setting.
exclude_ids	You can supply a comma separated list of friend ids, which will be excluded from the auto drop-down box.
prefill_ids	A comma separated list of friend ids, which will be selected automatically when this box is viewed.
prefill_locked	If set to true, the user cannot remove the prefilled friends.

Now, we will see how to manage the data that the user inputs. If your form contains multi-friend input, once submitted, you will find all theIDs of the selected friends in $_POST['ids'] or $_GET['ids']

```
<fb:multi-friend-input width="300px" border_color="#000"
                       exclude_ids="some id, another id" />
```

So, No Work For You?

Right, you have nothing else to do to send invitations except design the input form. That's the easiest thing ever, huh?

fb:application-name

This FBML tag helps you to easily define the name of your application, especially when it contains some restricted words in it, such as "message". As Facebook limits the usage of these restricted words when these invitations go to news feed and mini feed, you can use fb:application-name to rescue them.

```
<fb:application-name>
Message builder
</fb:application-name>
```

Notifications

Notifications are another important thing for Facebook developers, using which they can send notifications to the users of their applications. There are two ways of using notifications:

- Notify the pages of users
- Email them

Sending notifications to the notification page of users does not require confirmation from users. So you can use this to send information about the activity of their friends who are also users of this application. You can also send notification to non-users of your applications, but that strictly depends on the spamminess of the message. Here's a nice article about how the spamminess of a notification has been measured `http://www.facebook.com/topic.php?uid=2205007948&topic=13262&start=30 &hash=0ce1d00dde55ae7fc1d6f206621bdfc4#post71908`.

In this section, we will show you how to send notifications to Facebook users. There are two functions in the Facebook REST API library for sending notifications:

- `notifications_send`
- `notifications_sendEmail`

notifications_send

As explained earlier, you can send notifications to the user's notifications page using this function. This page is located at `http://www.facebook.com/notifications. php`. Let's have a look at the following code, which sends invitations to your application. This function supports two parameters. The first one is an array of users to whom you want to send notifications. The next one is a text block (could be FMBL block too), which can contain only text and links.

```php
<?php
include_once("prepend.php");
$facebook->api_client->notifications_send(array(503274632),"This is a
sample Notification from Facebook Application Development Book");
?>
```

You remember what the content of `prepend.php` was? Please take a look at the previous chapter.

Now, the output is interesting like the following one:

> **Today**
>
> - ☐ Hasin Hayder This is a sample Notification from Facebook   ✗
>   Application Development Book 11:19pm
>
> 🖐 Mehedy Kabir has high fiiiived you. High five, wish 'Happy New   ✗
>   Year' to, or dance with Mehedy! ... OR SuperPoke back! 9:46pm
>
> 💬 Ahmed Muztaba just sent you a message. Click here to read   ✗
>   your message 6:22pm
>
> 💬 Hasan Sagor just sent you a message. Click here to read your   ✗
>   message 4:53pm

The top one is the one we have just sent.

Limitation

You can send a maximum of 40 invitations to a user of your application per day.

notifications_sendEmail

This function is used for sending notifications to a user's mailbox, instead of the notification page. Emails are much more effective than the notification page, and that's why there is a greater chance of spamming. Facebook allows you to send a maximum number of 5 emails per user, per day. notifications_sendEmail needs the user's permission before you finally dispatch the mail. Let's take a look:

This function accepts four parameters. The first one is an array of users whom you want to email. The second one is the subject of the email. Third one is the content in plain text, and the fourth one is the content in HTML. This function returns a comma separated list of all successful recipients. Let's have a look at the following code block:

```
<div style="padding:20px;">
    <?php
    if (empty($_POST['ids'])){
    ?>
    <form method="POST">
    Please Select Some friends whom you want to send an Email.
        <fb:multi-friend-input width="300px" border_color="#000"
include_me='true' exclude_ids="" /><br/>
    Please type something to them<br/>
```

```
<textarea name ='email'></textarea><br/>
<input type='submit' value='Send Mail' />
</form>
    <?}?>
</div>
<div style="padding:20px;">
    <?php
    include_once("prepend.php");
    if (!empty($_POST['ids'])){
    $email = $_POST['email'];
    $successful_friends= $facebook->api_client->notifications_
sendEmail($_POST['ids'],"This is a sample Mail from Facebook
Application Development Book",$email,$email);
    echo "Emails successfully sent to the following friends <br/>";
    $parts = explode(",",$successful_friends);
    foreach($parts as $part)
    echo "<fb:name uid='{$part}' useyou='false' /></br>";
    }
    ?>
</div>
```

When you run it, it will show something like this:

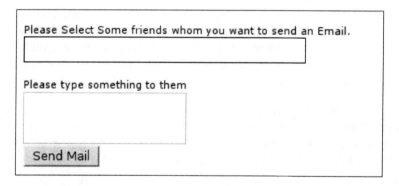

Now, if you type some friends' names in the friends input box, some content in the mail box, and then hit the send button, you will get a screen like this:

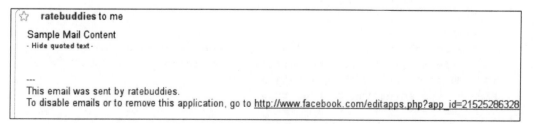

And the mail content in your mailbox will look like this:

```
Emails successfully sent to the following friends
Hasin Hayder
Manzil Monabber Tantra
```

Tips for Effective Notification and Emailing

As notification and emails are an effective way of keeping your users up to date as well as promoting your application, you should use them carefully to take maximum advantage of them. Here are some tips for successful promotion:

- Catch the most interesting moments of your application, and ask your users to send emails to their friends before it. For example, if you are creating a quiz application, after displaying the result to your user who has taken the quiz just now, display an invite page. Most of the users invite their friends in such cases. In the email you are sending, you can send the score of that user which makes his invitation more colorful.

- As soon as someone installs your application, show them an invitation page before they dive further.

- Keep some links such as "Show your performance/score/whatever to your friends", which redirect your users to an invitation page when clicked.

- Whenever a user has achieved or done something interesting, send his friends (who are also the users of this application) some notifications.

- Use notifications to send updates of your application to the users of your application.

- You can keep a page in your application, where a user can monitor the activities of his friends for that application. Also, display a "congratulate your friend" link, which can be used to send emails.

- Use your creativity.

Summary

This chapter taught you how to build an invitation system along with notification and emails. Popularity of a Facebook application depends very much on how effectively you can promote your application to as many users as you can. So use notifications and emails effectively throughout your application. While doing this, also take care of spamminess, so that you don't get blocked.

8
Photos

The last chapter taught us how to create a notification and invitation system using Facebook's notification APIs. In this chapter, we will discuss how to use Facebook's photo APIs to make some interesting stuff. We will also learn the details of Facebook's group and event APIs. So, more or less, this chapter will show us the following:

- Creating a photo importer from Facebook
- Creating a slideshow application
- Letting viewers upload photos to your album.

Photo API

Facebook is extremely popular, especially because it gives us the facility to upload photos on to the Facebook server. Facebook is now one of the major photo-sharing services along with Flickr and Photobucket. Most surprisingly, Facebook allows you to share photos from Facebook with non-Facebook users. In this section, we will show you how you can play with these Photo APIs:

For getting started the tasks successfully completed, we will use the following photo functions provided by Facebook:

- `photos_getAlbums`
- `photos_getTags`
- `photos_get`
- `photos_upload`
- `photos_addTag`
- `photos_createAlbum`

Note that:

The REST library for PHP5 developers contains only the first three functions. So, we will create the rest.

`photos_addTag` can be used only on pending photos.

There are size restrictions for photo albums. Regular albums can contain a maximum of 60 pictures, and a default album can contain up to 1,000 pictures.

photos_getAlbum

This function helps application developers to retrieve all the photo albums belonging to a specific user. It takes two parameters:

Parameter	What is it?
Uid	User id of the user whose album info you are trying to retrieve.
Aids	This is an optional array where you can specify album ids that you are particularly interested in.

Let's implement this function to understand how it works, and the details of the return values. I am using my user ID in this example.

```php
<?php
    include_once("prepend.php");
    echo "Here is all your photo albums";
    echo "<pre>";
    print_r($facebook->api_client->photos_getAlbums(503274632));
    echo "</pre>";
?>.
```

This will display the following information:

```
Array
(
    [0] => Array
        (
            [aid] => 2161548085346438750
            [cover_pid] => 2161548085346730648
            [owner] => 503274632
            [name] => Me Myself
```

```
            [created] => 1189199787
            [modified] => 1199389617
            [description] => Me Myself
            [location] =>
            [link] => http://www.facebook.com/album.php?aid=3678&id=5
03274632
            [size] => 6
        )

    )
```

So, you got all the information about my (well, any user actually) albums for further processing. What you can do now is retrieve all the photos in this album.

```php
<?
include_once("prepend.php");

//Retrieve the list of albums those belong to this user
$albums = $facebook->api_client->photos_getAlbums('503274632',null);

//Now loop through each album
foreach ($albums as $album){

//Retrieve all the photos belong to current album
    $photos = $facebook->api_client->photos_get(null,
                                        $album['aid'],null);

//Loop through each photo
    foreach ($photos as $photo)
    {

//Display current photo
        echo "<img src='{$photo['src_small']}' vspace=10 /><br/> {$photo
['caption']}<br/>";
    }
}
?>
```

Accessing from an External Application

Importing Facebook Photos from an external web application is a bit tough and you should have a proper knowledge about the Facebook authentication system to do it. In this section, we will look at importing pictures from an external page.

But before you run your external code, you must associate it with any of your Facebook Applications, by providing the API and Secret key of that application. You can go to `http://www.facebook.com/developers/editapp.php?new` to set up a new application if you don't have any.

Required Fields

Application Name
(Limit: 50 characters)

booksaholic

▼ **Optional Fields**

Base options

Support E-mail
(Limit: 100 characters)

countdraculla@gmail.com

We will contact you at this address if there are any problems or important updates.

Callback Url
(Limit: 100 characters)

http://javapark.net/hasin/fb/desktop/

After logging into Facebook, users are redirected to the callback URL. See authentication overview for more details.

Canvas Page URL

http://apps.facebook.com/booksaholic /

⦿ Use FBML ⦿ Use iframe

Your application will be viewable in the Facebook navigation at this URL - either as rendered FBML or loaded in an iframe. If you aren't sure what you should use here, choose FBML. You can use iframes within FBML on canvas pages with the <fb:iframe> tag, and most things you will want to do will be easier and faster with FBML.

Application Type

⦿ Website ⦿ Desktop

Mobile Integration

☐ My application uses the mobile platform

Checking this will enable some additional SMS functionality for applications.

IP Addresses of Servers Making Requests
(comma-separated)

If you supply this information (e.g. 10.1.20.1, 10.1.20.3), requests from addresses other than those listed will be rejected.

Can your application be added on Facebook?

⦿ Yes ⦿ No

Select Yes if your application can be added to a Facebook account.

TOS URL

The URL pointing to your application's Terms of Service, which the user must accept.

Developers: booksaholic

Type a friend's name

Icon ☐

Change your icon

Displayed in the left menu of Facebook if the application has been added in the user's profile.

Save or Cancel

And after you get your API key, the settings page should look like the previous example. For this example, my application name is **booksaholic**.

Now, we will code an external page to grab some photos from our Facebook profiles. When someone runs this page for the first time, they will get a login screen, and will be prompted if they want to allow this application to access their information, and install it to their profile.

```php
<?php
include_once("facebook.php");

$apiKey = "api key";
$secretKey = "secret key";
$facebook= new Facebook($apiKey,$secretKey);
$fbuser= $facebook->require_login();
//get all the albums of this user
$albums = $facebook->api_client->photos_getAlbums($fbuser,null);
//loop through each of these albums
foreach ($albums as $album){
    $photos = $facebook->api_client->photos_get(null,$album['aid'],nul
l);
    foreach ($photos as $photo)
    {
        echo "<img src='{$photo['src_small']}' vspace=10 /><br/> {$photo
['caption']}<br/>";
    }
}
?>
```

If the viewer of this page is not a user of the application, they will immediately get a login screen, as shown here. Then, if they log in, our script will be able to fetch data.

Well, as you get access to all those pictures, you can access all your photos on Facebook, and use them any way you want.

Uploading Photo

This is a challenging part for Facebook developers—to upload photos to a user's album. Jeremy Blanchard, Paul Wells, and Kevin Pazirandeh at http://eyermonkey. com provided a solution by creating a photo upload library. You can download the latest code from http://eyermonkey.com/files/facebook_php5_photoslib.zip and unzip it. You will get a file named facebook_php5_photoslib.php.

The following code will upload a photo in your first album:

```php
<?php
require_once 'facebook_php5_photoslib.php';

$appapikey = 'api key';
$appsecret = 'secret key';
$facebook = new FacebookPhotos($appapikey, $appsecret);
$user = $facebook->require_login();

// list of albums
$albums = $facebook->api_client->photos_getAlbums($user, null);

// Pick the first album for sake of the example
$aid = $albums[0]['aid'];

$filename = 'http://images.packtpub.com/images/full/1847192564.jpg';
$caption = 'OOP with PHP5, My Latest Book';

// now upload it
$upload_result = $facebook->api_client->photos_upload($filename, $aid,
$caption);

// result
echo '<pre>';
print_r($upload_result);
echo '</pre>';
?>
```

This code will output like this

```
Array
(
    [pid] => 2161548085346738070
    [aid] => 2161548085346438750
    [owner] => 503274632
    [src] => http://photos-c.ak.facebook.com/photos-ak-sf2p/
v166/93/78/503274632/s503274632_302998_6409.jpg
```

```
    [src_big] => http://photos-c.ak.facebook.com/photos-ak-sf2p/
v166/93/78/503274632/n503274632_302998_6409.jpg
    [src_small] => http://photos-c.ak.facebook.com/photos-ak-sf2p/
v166/93/78/503274632/t503274632_302998_6409.jpg
    [link] => http://www.facebook.com/
                                    photo.php?pid=302998&id=503274632
    [caption] => OOP with PHP5, My Latest Book
    [created] => 1199709406
)
```

As soon you run this code and go back to your first album in Facebook, you will see that Facebook shows you this status:

Now, if you go inside your album, it will ask for your permission to add the newly uploaded photo to your albums.

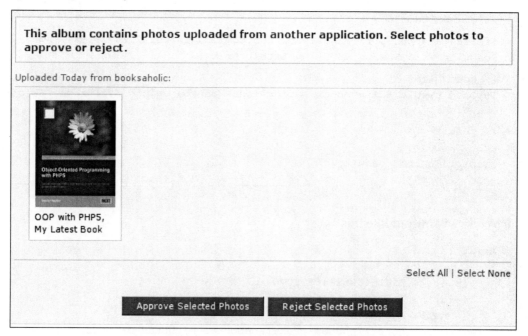

You can now click on the photo, and check this checkbox, and then click on **Approve Selected Photos**. It will be added to your album right away.

You can use this application to import all your photos from Flickr, Photobucket or other popular photo-sharing services, and upload them to Facebook. In the next section, we will create a nice application that will enable you to add a slideshow of all the photos in your profile. But before that, let's have a look at something different.

Tagging Your Photos

The library we just created lacks the feature to tag a photo.

 Tagging means you can mark a photo with a set of tags i.e. meaningful words, which will help others to search based on those tags.

So, we will add the support of `photos_addTag` and play with that. Let's have a look at the following code. We will add this function inside `facebook_php5_photoslib.php`:

```php
function addTag($pid, $uid, $text, $x, $y, $tags)
{
    return $this->call_method('facebook.photos.addTag',
      array(
      'pid' => $pid,
      'tag_uid' => $uid,
      'tag_text' => $text,
      'x' => $x,
      'y' => $y,
      'tags' => $tags));
}
```

And here comes an example for using this. The following code uploads a photo and tags it:

```php
<?php
require_once 'facebook_php5_photoslib.php';
$appapikey = 'ff0b3d87fc42915533e15dc238f2d447';
$appsecret = 'secret key';
$facebook = new FacebookPhotos($appapikey, $appsecret);
$user = $facebook->require_login();
// list of albums
$albums = $facebook->api_client->photos_getAlbums($user, null);
// Pick the first album for sake of the example
$aid = $albums[0]['aid'];
$filename = 'http://images.packtpub.com/images/full/1847192564.jpg';
$caption = 'OOP with PHP5, My Latest Book';
```

```
// now upload it
$upload_result = $facebook->api_client->photos_upload($filename, $aid,
$caption);

//now add the tag
$tag = $facebook->api_client->addTag($upload_result['pid'],503274632,"
OOP with PHP5",25,25,null);
echo '<pre>';
print_r($tag);
echo '</pre>';
?>
```

You will see the output as 1, which means that the code was successful. But let's have a look at the album. Now, it says that your photo contains a tag in it.

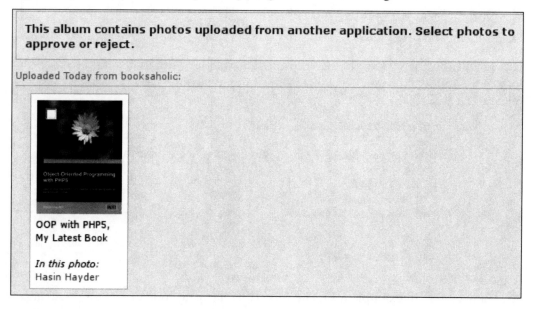

So basically, that's it!

Slideshow Application

In this section, we will develop a cool slideshow application that will create stunning slideshows from all the pictures in your album. Then, you can set this inside your profile. Let's have a look at the following list to understand what we need for this:

- A Flash-based slideshow component
- Some introductory knowledge to Facebook's FBML tags for embedding Flash.

For the slideshow, we will use the free slideshow component from Maani.us
`http://maani.us/slideshow/index.php?menu=Introduction`.

After downloading, extract `slideshow.php` and `slideshow.swf` from the archive in
the same directory where you will place your code.

Let's have a look at the following code. I took all the images of this slideshow from
Flickr. The following code makes a fantastic slideshow, which we are going to use in
our Facebook application. Here is the code that generates the necessary XML data for
our slideshow component:

```php
//sample.php
<?php

//include slideshow.php in your script
include "slideshow.php";

//add 3 slides
$slideshow[ 'slide' ][ 0 ] = array ( 'url' => "images/2150941247_
c0819d6df5_b.jpg" );
$slideshow[ 'slide' ][ 1 ] = array ( 'url' => "images/2152121556_
74309809f8_b.jpg" );
$slideshow[ 'slide' ][ 2 ] = array ( 'url' => "images/2155472115_
b0e6f24b0d_b.jpg" );
$slideshow[ 'slide' ][ 3 ] = array ( 'url' => "images/2156352894_
54f9660033_o.jpg" );
$slideshow[ 'slide' ][ 4 ] = array ( 'url' => "images/2158603834_
9a42879650_b.jpg" );
$slideshow[ 'slide' ][ 5 ] = array ( 'url' => "images/2159242529_
7c6bc73591_b.jpg" );

$slideshow[ 'transition' ][ 0 ] = array ( 'type' => "drop", 'duration'
=> 1 );
$slideshow[ 'transition' ][ 1 ] = array ( 'type' => "fade_to_black",
'duration' => 2 );
$slideshow[ 'transition' ][ 2 ] = array ( 'type' => "push_up",
'duration' => 1 );
$slideshow[ 'transition' ][ 3 ] = array ( 'type' => "spin", 'duration'
=> 1 );
$slideshow[ 'transition' ][ 4 ] = array ( 'type' => "fade_to_white",
'duration' => 2 );
$slideshow[ 'transition' ][ 5 ] = array ( 'type' => "reveal_right",
'duration' => 1 );

//send the slideshow data
Send_Slideshow_Data ( $slideshow );

?>
```

Now let's make use of it:

```
<HTML>
<BODY bgcolor="#FFFFFF">
<?php
//include slideshow.php to access the Insert_Slideshow function
include "slideshow.php";

//insert the slideshow.swf flash file into the web page
//tell slideshow.swf to get the slideshow's data from sample.php
created in the first step
//set the slideshow's width to 320 pixels and the height to 240
echo Insert_Slideshow ( "slideshow.swf", "sample.php", 320, 240 );
?>
</BODY>
</HTML>
```

It gives you a nice slideshow like the following one, with excellent transition effects:

That's indeed a very nice slideshow! Now we are going to use it in our Facebook application. Let's have a look at the following code:

```
//http://apps.facebook.com/booksaholic/slide.php
<?php
include_once("facebook.php");

$apiKey = "api key";
$secretKey = "secret key";

$facebook= new Facebook($apiKey,$secretKey);
$fbuser= $facebook->require_login();

//get all the albums and photos belong to those album

$albums = $facebook->api_client->photos_getAlbums($fbuser,null);

foreach ($albums as $album){
    $photos = $facebook->api_client->photos_get(null,$album['aid'],nul
l);
    $images = array();
    foreach ($photos as $photo)
    {
        $images[]= $photo['src_big'];
    }
}

//write the serialize format of these images in a text file for later
use
file_put_contents("data/{$fbuser}.srz",serialize($images));

//prepare the URLs needed by the slideshow component, you can see
details of this component in maani.us
$url1 = urlencode("http://javapark.net/hasin/fb/desktop/slides.
php?id={$fbuser}");
$url = "http://javapark.net/hasin/fb/desktop/slideshow.swf?stage_
width=320&stage_height=240&php_source={$url1}";
?>

<?
//display the slideshow component as flash

$str = <<<EOD
<div style='padding:20px;'>
    <fb:swf          swfbgcolor='#000' swfsrc='{$url}' width='320'
height='240' imgsrc='{$images[1]}' />
</div>
EOD;
if ($_POST['add']=="Yes")
{
    $facebook->api_client->profile_setFBML('',$fbuser,$str);
}
echo $str;
?>
```

```
<!--ask user if they want to display the slideshow on their profile-->
<div style='padding:20px;'>
    <fb:editor action="" labelwidth="100">
        <b>Do you want to set this in your profile?</b>
        <fb:editor-buttonset>
            <fb:editor-button value="Yes" name="add"/>
            <fb:editor-button value="No" name="add"/>
        </fb:editor-buttonset>
    </fb:editor>
</div>
```

The above code actually retrieves all the images from all the albums of the logged-in user, and stores them in the form of a serialized array in the `data/{$fbuser}.srz` file. The following file then retrieves this data and creates the necessary XML for slideshow:

```php
//slides.php
<?
//this code prepare the slides as XML data to use with slideshow
component
include_once("slideshow.php");
$fbuser = $_GET['id'];
$data = file_get_contents("data/{$fbuser}.srz");
$images = unserialize($data);
makeSlideshow($images);

function makeSlideshow($images)
{
    $slideshow = array();
    foreach ($images as $image)
    {
        $slideshow[ 'slide' ][] = array("url"=>$image);
        $slideshow[ 'transition' ][] = array ( 'type' => "fade_to_
white", 'duration' => 2 );
    }
    Send_Slideshow_Data ( $slideshow );
}
?>
```

Here is the output of `slides.php`. This XML data is processed by the slideshow component, and displays it as a slideshow.

```
<slideshow>
        <slide>
                <image url="http://photos-b.ak.facebook.com/photos-ak-
sf2p/v132/93/78/503274632/n503274632_94889_7682.jpg" />
```

```
                <transition type="fade_to_white" duration="2" />
        </slide>

        <slide>
                <image url="http://photos-c.ak.facebook.com/photos-ak-
sf2p/v117/93/78/503274632/n503274632_94890_1536.jpg" />
                <transition type="fade_to_white" duration="2" />
        </slide>

        <slide>
                <image url="http://photos-a.ak.facebook.com/photos-ak-
sf2p/v159/93/78/503274632/n503274632_295576_7381.jpg" />
                <transition type="fade_to_white" duration="2" />
        </slide>

        <slide>
                <image url="http://photos-c.ak.facebook.com/photos-ak-
sf2p/v166/93/78/503274632/n503274632_302998_6409.jpg" />
                <transition type="fade_to_white" duration="2" />
        </slide>

</slideshow>
```

And, here is the output of `http://apps.facebook.com/booksaholic/slide.php`.

Now, if you click on **Yes**, it will set the slideshow in your profile.

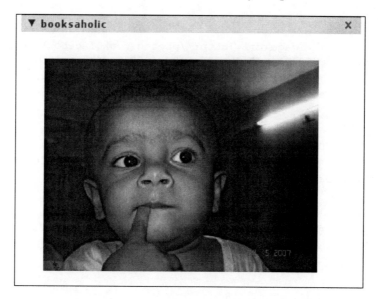

Summary

In this chapter, we learned how to do cool things using Facebook's photo API. Now, using them, you can easily develop a Facebook to Blog Importer, or Facebook to Flickr Importer, or Facebook Photo Mailer, a Photo Editor or whatever wild things you can imagine. This section also helped us understand the photo uploading from external applications, and the authentication system for external applications.

In the next chapter, we will learn about Facebook tools to create some discussion groups, comments section, attachments, and walls. That will be another exciting chapter.

9

Tools and Multimedia

In the previous chapter, we saw how to use the photo APIs of Facebook and create some interesting stuff. Besides that, Facebook provides excellent tools to manage user input using some built-in tools for application developers. In this chapter, we will discuss in detail Facebook tools for user input and interaction. Using these tools, you can take feedback from users, create discussion forums, create walls, and send attachments.

In the coming sections, we will learn how to use the following tags effectively and make an interesting project using them:

- `fb:board`
- `fb:comments`
- `fb:google-analytics`
- `fb:typeahed-input`
- `fb:user-agent`
- `fb:wall`
- `fb:share-button`
- `fb:random`
- `fb:switch`

Creating a Discussion Board

Application developers might need to create discussion boards in their application. To create one from scratch, with all the nice functionalities that Facebook provides, is really a time consuming process. That's why Facebook provides a nice FBML tag `fb:board` for application developers to take full advantage of. In this section, we will create a discussion board, and show how to modify the default UI.

The following code will help you to instantly plug-in a discussion board in your application so that people can also use it right away. Let's have a look at the following code:

```php
<?php
include_once("facebook.php");
$apiKey = "api key";
$secretKey = "secret key";
$facebook= new Facebook($apiKey,$secretKey);
$fbuser= $facebook->require_login();
?>
<div style='padding:20px;'>
    <fb:board xid="Sample_Board_for_Facebook_Application_Developers"
canpost="true"
candelete="false"
canmark="true"
cancreatetopic="true"
numtopics="10" >
    <fb:title>Sample board for facebook application developers</fb:
title>
    </fb:board>
</div>
```

This will output the following blank discussion board:

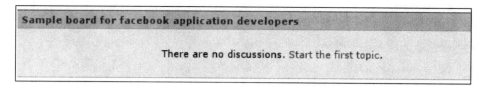

When visitors click on **Start the first topic**, they will be redirected to a new page:

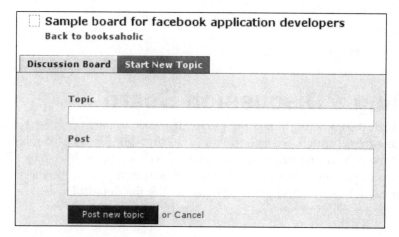

And after submitting this form with contents, users will be redirected to the topics page to display the post you have just made.

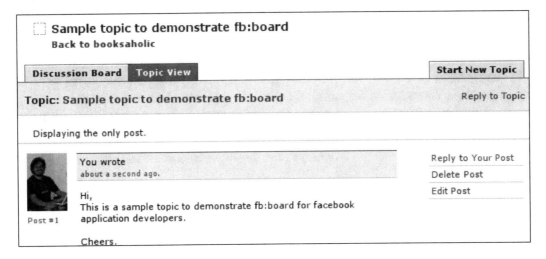

And now you can take a look at your discussion page once again. It is now displaying the topic you have just posted.

So that is fun, right? You write a simple `<fb:board />` tag, and it creates the whole discussion board and manages its functionalities for you.

Let's have a look at the parameters of this excellent FBML tag.

Parameter	What does it do?
xid	A unique identifier for your board. It can contain alphabets, numbers, and underscore. This has to be unique for your board. So, you can use proper name space with the name.
canpost	If set to true, viewers can post in your board. Otherwise, it is read-only.
candelete	When set to true, users will be able to delete any topic of this board.
canmark	Users will be able to mark a post as relevant or irrelevant if set to true.
cancreatetopic	If set to true, users will be able to create new topics.
numtopics	Number of topics to display in the first page.
callbackurl	This is used to re-fetch this configuration.
returnurl	This is used to redirect a user when he/she clicks on the **back** link.

Application developers can use the `<fb:title>` tag inside a `<fb:board>` to display the corresponding title as we did in the previous example.

Taking Comments from Users

In this section, we are going to create a wall to take user feedback on a specific topic. This won't be as vast as `fb:board` by functionalities, but it will serve its purpose really well. Facebook provides an excellent FBML tag named `fb:comments`, for application developers, to ease this process. This comment box is useful for taking instant user feedback just under a selected resource (image, media files, or articles).

To understand how to use the comment box, let's have a look at the following code:

```
<?
//necessary authentication, see the previous example
?>
<div style="padding:20px">
<!-- The following Image is taken from Flickr Interesting Photo Sets-->
    <img src="http://farm3.static.flickr.com/2262/2187180980_
a7afc96621.jpg?v=0" vspace="10" />
    <div>
        <fb:comments
                xid=»some_comments_about_lemon_juice»
                canpost=»true»
                candelete=»false»

returnurl=»http://apps.facebook.com/booksaholic/comments.php»>
            <fb:title>How about some fresh lemon juice?</fb:title>
        </fb:comments>
    </div>
</div>
```

This will output the following comment board on your page:

Now, your users can post their feedback directly under it. Let's make some comments and see how it looks.

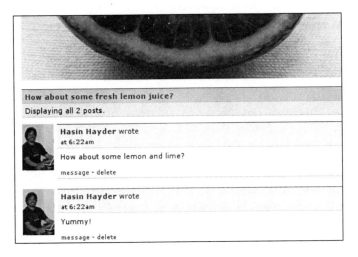

So that's it! Using Facebook's `fb:comment`, you can manage user feedback anywhere. Let's have a look at the parameters of this fantastic tag:

Parameter	What does it do?
`xid`	A unique identifier for your comment board. It can contain alphabets, numbers, and underscore.
`canpost`	If set to true, viewers can post in your comment board. Otherwise, it is read-only.
`candelete`	When set to true, users will be able to delete any topic of this comment board.
`numposts`	Number of comments to display in this board.
`callbackurl`	After a successful comment is made, Facebook will call this URL with all the details. So, this will be the appropriate place to count comments for a specific comment board.
`returnurl`	This is used to redirect a user when he or she clicks on the **back** link.
`showform`	If it is set to true, users will stay in the same page after posting a comment. Otherwise, they will be redirected to the **See All Comments** page.
`send_notification_uid`	If set, Facebook will drop a mail to the email address of this user when a comment is made.

If you are not sure how to count the number of comments for a specific topic, you can place the following code in your application or server-side code:

```
//Check if comments are submitted
if(isset($_POST['fb_sig_xid_action'])){

$action = $_POST['fb_sig_xid_action'];

//Determine if it's deleting or adding to the comments
if($action == 'delete'){
 $count = -1;
}else{
 $count = 1;
}
//now write this counter somewhere to keep track
}
```

To track multiple boards, first check which board is submitted using the `$_POST['xid']` parameter.

Making a Wall Using fb:wall

Besides Facebook's automated comment and discussion board system, if you want to make your own and display them with a Facebook flavor, you can simulate the look-n-feel using the `fb:wall` and `fb:wallposts` tags. In this section, we will show you how:

```
<div style='padding:20px;'>
    <fb:wall>
        <fb:wallpost uid="698645856">  This is a sample wall post
simulated using fb:wall and fb:wallpost
        </fb:wallpost>
    </fb:wall>
</div>
```

Note that `fb:wallpost` must be inside a `fb:wall` tag. This code creates a screen as follows:

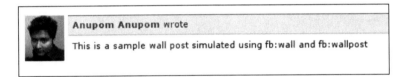

So, `fb:wall` and `fb:wallpost` are basically used to simulate all the content in the Facebook style. It doesn't serve any other goal. Let's have a look at their parameters.

Parameter	What does it do?
uid	User ID to display the corresponding photo as a poster.
t	Time stamp in UNIX epoch to display under post title.

If you supply `t`, it will look like the following:

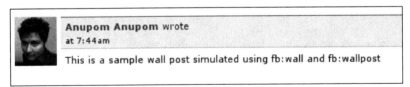

And the code was:

```
<div style='padding:20px;'>
    <fb:wall>
        <fb:wallpost uid="698645856" t='<?=time();?>'>  This is a sample
wall post simulated using fb:wall and fb:wallpost
        </fb:wallpost>
    </fb:wall>
</div>
```

Besides fb:wall and fb;wallpost, there is another wall tag—fb:wallpost-action. This tag must be inside fb:wall, and is used to display an anchor (text link) inside the wall post. It supports only one parameter, that is, href, and takes a URL. Let's have a look at the following example:

```
<div style='padding:20px;'>
    <fb:wall>
        <fb:wallpost uid="698645856" t='<?=time();?>'>  This is a sample
wall post simulated using fb:wall and fb:wallpost
        </fb:wallpost>
        <fb:wallpost-action href='http://google.com'>Search anything in
great Google</fb:wallpost-action>

    </fb:wall>
</div>
```

Increasing Usability Using fb:switch

Facebook provides another very good tool to smoothen the user experience and that is the typeahead tool (you can think of it as an auto-complete text box). It looks like a simple text box. But, when the user starts typing in it, it automatically provides suggestions below the text box, for the user to pick the best option.

This tag also makes use of another tag with which you can define all the options —fb:typeahead-option.

Before using this tag, let's have a look at the constraints:

- This tag must be wrapped in a fb:fbml tag with version 1.1.
- You must give a name to the input box, you cannot keep it blank.
- You must set autocomplete="off" to prevent the browser's auto-complete from overriding that of the tag.

Let's have a look at the following piece of code, which shows us how to use this tool:

```
<fb:fbml version="1.1">
    <div style='padding:20px; height:700px;'>
    Please select your country by typing here: <br/>
        <fb:typeahead-input name="country" autocomplete="off">
        <?php
        $data = file_get_contents("http://javapark.net/hasin/fb/desktop/
countries.xml");
        $sxml = simplexml_load_string($data);
        foreach ($sxml->country as $country)
        {
            $countryname =$country."";
            echo "<fb:typeahead-option value='{$country['code']}'>{$count
ryname}</fb:typeahead-option>   ";
        }
        ?>
        </fb:typeahead-input>
    </div>
</fb:fbml>
```

And this will create a nice typeahead tool for country names. Take a look at the following screenshot:

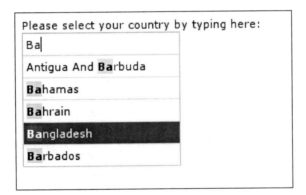

When submitted, you can capture the user input from the post variable "country" as $_POST['country']. So basically, this typeahead tool behaves just like a normal input element.

Using fb:random to Display a Random Option

Using `fb:random` and `fb:random-option` together, you can display a random item from a given set of options. In `fb:random-option`, you can also specify weights. Items with higher weights are subjected to appear more frequently than those of lower weights.

`fb:random` takes two parameters as shown here:

Parameters	What does it do?
Pick	Number of items to choose from the given list. Its default value is 1.
Unique	If you set it to true, all the items chosen from the list will remain unique with no duplicates.

Let's see an example:

```
In "Thinner the winner Game" the winner is:
<fb:random>
    <fb:random-option weight= '2'>Mr X Weighs 240 Lb (Less chance to
win)</fb:random-option>
    <fb:random-option weight= '1'>Mr X Weighs 150 Lb (More chance to
win)</fb:random-option>
</fb:random>
```

Increasing Usability Using fb:switch

In Facebook, contents are restricted to the users in the network; hence all content is not visible to everyone. So, if you try to display something to a set of users, for example a photo, the users who are not in the network may not see it. In this case, `fb:swith` acts like a saver. It takes some option inside this tag, and evaluates the first one to display that content. So, for example, let's consider that you want to display a specific photo to your application users. If they cannot view it, they will see their profile photo.

Here's a tiny example taken from Facebook wiki. Here, if the user has the rights to display the picture specified by pid, then he will see the picture. Else, if he has the rights to display the profile picture, it will be shown to him. If he doesn't have the right to see any of these, he will see the text as "You can't see either the photo or the profile pic".

```
<fb:switch>
    <fb:photo pid="12345" />
    <fb:profile-pic uid="54321" />
    <fb:default>You can't see either the photo or the profile pic</fb:
default>
</fb:switch>
```

Sharing Content

Facebook provides a nifty tool for application developers to let their users share content with everyone. Using this tool, any user can post the content in his or her profile. If you are not sure how to do it, we will do that using the `fb:share-button` tag. Using this tag, you can share textual and multimedia content with your friends as well as publish in your profile. This tag makes extensive use of `meta` and `link` tags. Let's have a look at the following lists to understand how to share different types of content.

`meta` tags in Facebook sharing buttons acts as if they are setting the values for some common attributes. For example, using `meta`, you can set the value of the title and description. When you need to link to external resources, you can make use of the `link` tag, and define the relation using the `rel` attribute.

You can share an article, or anything using the following format:

```
<fb:share-button>
<meta name="medium" content="medium_type" />
<meta name="title" content="Title of this article" />
<meta name="description" content="Your Content" />
<link rel="image_src" href="any attached image url" />
</fb:share-button>
```

The valid medium types are `audio`, `video`, `image`, `mult`, `news`, and `blog`.

Let's have a look at the following code that shares an image:

```
<fb:share-button class="meta">
    <meta name="medium" content="blog"/>
    <meta name="title" content="Need for Speed Prostreet"/>
    <meta name="description" content="VW R32"/>

    <link rel="image_src" href="http://www.ea.com/downloads/eagames/
nfs/prostreet/content/img/rollout3/vw_r32.jpg" />
    <link rel="target_url" href="http://apps.facebook.com/
needforspeed/preview.php?id=124" />
</fb:share-button>
```

We placed such links, just below the images, in one of our applications (`http://apps.facebook.com/needforspeed`) and it looks like the following:

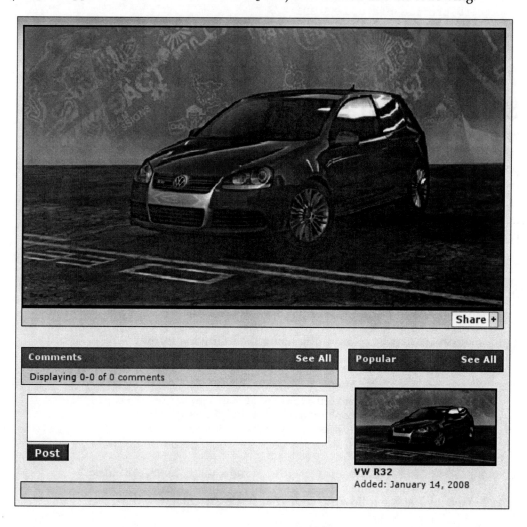

When you click on the **Share** button, it will show you a screen like the following one:

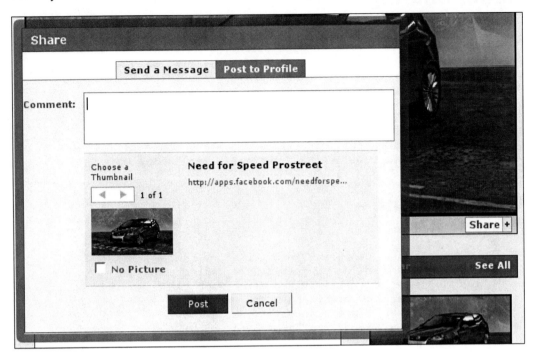

Now, you can write anything, and click **Post,** and it will appear in your profile. You can also choose **Send a Message,** instead of **Post to Profile,** from the top bar. When published, it will look like the following one in the mini-feed section in your profile:

Audio Sharing

The following example code will show you how to share an audio content:

```
<meta name="title" content="page_title" />
<meta name="description" content="audio_description" />
<link rel="image_src" href="audio_image_src url (eg. album art)" />
<link rel="audio_src" href="audio_src url" />

<meta name="audio_title" content="audio_title (eg. song name)" />
<meta name="audio_artist" content="audio_artist_name" />
<meta name="audio_album" content="audio_album_name" />
<meta name="audio_type" content="Content-Type header field" />
```

Video Sharing

The format is like this:

```
<meta name="title" content="video_title" />
<meta name="description" content="video_description" />
<link rel="image_src" href="video_screenshot_image_src url" />
<link rel="video_src" href="video_src url"/>*
<meta name="video_height" content="video_height" />
<meta name="video_width" content="video_width" />
<meta name="video_type" content="Content-Type header field" />
```

Multimedia Contents

Facebook provides a set of FBML tags to handle multimedia content in Facebook applications. These tags make a developer's life really easier. You can do almost anything that can be done, using these tags. But sometimes, they might not seem enough. In this section, we will learn how to use these tags, and what the exceptions are. If you are planning to develop an application with multimedia content, you will find this section really useful.

To manage image, audio, video, and flash contents, FBML provides the following tags:

- `fb:photo`: To display photos uploaded by users.
- `fb:mp3`: To play an mp3 file using an audio player.
- `fb:flv`: To display a default flv player.
- `fb:swf`: To play a flash movie (swf file) using a built-in Flash player.

If you want to display a flash movie using the fb:flv tag, then please keep in mind that it is always displayed in a square size. So, if your movie is in a wide screen format, you can use the JW FLV player that we've used later in our example. It's an open-source player free for non-commercial use, and costs 15 USD for commercial use.

Displaying Photo

Using the fb:photo tag, you can display photo in a canvas and in the profile box. Using this tag is easy. You just need to be aware of some small issues.

fb:photo tag takes the following four parameters:

Parameter	What does it do?
pid	This is the ID of a specific photo returned from an API call or an FQL query. It can also be the ID from the browser query string. There are slight differences in display in both these cases. Take a look at the note that follows the table.
uid	The user ID that this photo belongs to.
size	Size of the photo. The default value is normal (n). Other supported values are small (s), square (q), and thumbnail (t).
align	The alignment of the photo could be left or right.

When you browse a photo of any user, take a look at the URL carefully. There are the user IDs and photo IDs available in that URL. For example, let's have a look at the following URL:

http://www.facebook.com/photo.php?pid=302998&l=dba66&id=503274632, which is a public URL to this photo.

You can display this photo anywhere in your application using photo tag like this:

```
<fb:photo pid='302998' uid='503274632'  size='t' />
```

But when you retrieve a photo from an API call or an FQL query, then those photo IDs are different from the previous ones, and you can directly display them using the `pid`. No `uid` is required. Let's have a look at the following returned value from a typical `photos.get()` call:

```
[0] => Array
        (
                [pid] => 2161548085346738070
                [aid] => 2161548085346438750
                [owner] => 503274632
                [src] => http://photos-g.ak.facebook.com/photos-ak-sf2p/
        v166/93/78/503274632/s503274632_302998_6409.jpg
                [src_big] => http://photos-g.ak.facebook.com/photos-ak-
        sf2p/v166/93/78/503274632/n503274632_302998_6409.jpg
                [src_small] => http://photos-g.ak.facebook.com/photos-ak-
        sf2p/v166/93/78/503274632/t503274632_302998_6409.jpg
                [link] => http://www.facebook.com/photo.php?pid=302998&id
        =503274632
                [caption] => OOP with PHP5, My Latest Book
                [created] => 1199709406
        )
```

This is the same photo that we used in our previous example. But look carefully, the `pid`s are different. Now, you can display this photo using only the `pid`, without the `uid`.

```
<fb:photo pid='2161548085346738070' />
```

Managing Audio

Using `fb:mp3`, you can embed a nifty audio player in your application. For the time being, this player can play only mp3 and no other format such as wmv. Moreover, please note that you have to point directly to the URL of your mp3 file, and not to URLs which do not end with .mp3. Please do remember that the file's bitrate must me in increments of 11KHz (11KHz, 22KHz, 44.1 KHz all work).

Using this tag in your application is simple. Take a look at the following code:

```
<fb:mp3 src="http://www.talkcrunch.com/mp3/Techcrunch-Ep001-
CalendarsAndEvents.mp3" title="Google Calendar v. the Competition"
artist="Nik Cubrilovic and Keith Teare" />
```

This will render the following mp3 player in your Facebook application canvas. The users see the following screenshot when they load this page:

The users gets to see the following one when they click play:

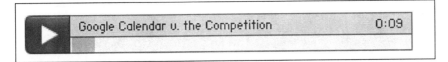

Basically, that is it! Let's have a look at the parameters:

Parameter	What does it do?
src	URL of the mp3 file
title	Title of the music
artist	The artist of the song
album	The album of the song
width	The width of the player
height	The height of the player

Managing Video (FLV Format)

Using fb:flv, you can embed an FLV player in your application. The only problem is that it always maintains the same aspect ratio. So you can't embed videos in a wide screen (16:10) format. If you embed them, they will be displayed in a rectangular mode, which will not produce the expected result. That's why, we have to use external players for the wide screen format. In this section, we will learn how to add FLV players using both fb:flv tag and an external player.

Embedding using fb:flv:

```
<div style='padding:20px;'>
<fb:flv src='http://www.youtube.com/get_video?video_id=D1R-jKKp3NA&t=O
EgsToPDskI3Qr5mDvxGrOd6TAbSRYRm' width='425' height='350' title='Steve
Jobs at Stanford' />
</div>
```

This will render a video player like the following one:

Let's have a look at the parameters:

Parameter	What does it do?
src	Url of the FLV file
title	Title of the video
width	The width of the player
height	The height of the player

If we are going to display FLVs using external players, you can use a very popular one that is free and open source, developed by Jeroen Wijering. It's available for downloading from `http://www.jeroenwijering.com/?item=JW_Media_Player`.

After downloading this player, unzip the archive, and upload the `mediaplayer.` `swf` in your web server. Then, we will use the `fb:swf` tag to display FLV using this player. Let's have a look at the following code:

```
<fb:swf allowfullscreen='true' swfbgcolor='#000000'
    flashvars='usefullscreen=false&file={$url_of_the_video}&displayHei
ght={$height}&image={$thumb}' height={$height} width={$width}
        swfsrc='{$path_to_mediaplayer.swf}' >
</fb:swf>
```

The most interesting feature is that it supports a preview image from the beginning. Let's have a look at the following screenshot taken from our NeedForSpeed application where we displayed these videos in a wide screen format:

Lets have a look at the parameters of the `fb:swf` tag:

Parameter	What does it do?
swfsrc	The URL of the Flash object. (The URL must be absolute.)
imgsrc	The URL of the image
width	The width of the image and the Flash object
height	The height of the image and the Flash object
imgstyle	The `style` attribute for the image
imgclass	The class attribute of the image
flashvars	The URL-encoded Flash variables
swfbgcolor	The hex-encoded background color for the Flash object

Parameter	What does it do?
waitforclick	Indicates whether to autoplay the Flash object (`false`), when allowed. `false` does not work in profiles for security and aesthetic reasons, except after an AJAX call (default value is true).
salign	The `salign` attribute; this is an `<embed>` parameter.
loop	Indicates whether to play the Flash object continuously.
quality	Indicates the quality of the object. Specify high, medium, or low.
scale	The scaling to apply to the object
align	Indicates how the browser aligns the object. Specify left, center, or right.
wmode	Indicates the opacity setting for the object. Specify transparent, opaque, or window.

Besides these, the following table shows you the flashvars automatically passed to the swf by Facebook.

Parameter	What does it do?
allowScriptAccess	This string is always set to `never`.
fb_sig_profile	The uid of the user into whose profile the Flash object is being loaded; this is blank when loaded in the canvas.
fb_sig_time	The time when the signature was generated
fb_sig_user	The uid of the currently logged-in user
fb_sig_session_key	The Facebook session key
fb_sig_expires	The session expiration time
fb_sig_api_key	Your application's API key
fb_sig_added	Indicates whether the user has added your application.
fb_sig	An MD5 hash of all the parameters with names that start with `fb_sig_` plus your application secret. This way, the Flash object can confirm that it is being loaded into a Facebook page. (But be careful while embedding your secret in your Flash application; hackers can get at it, if you do.)

Summary

This chapter helps application developers to understand all the necessary tags for embedding nice tools to interact with the users of their applications. Giving the highest priority to user interaction, Facebook provides these nifty tags to allow RAD (Rapid-Application-Development) for application developers. Besides these, we have also learned how to make nice applications with the help of multimedia tags.

Index

Thank you for buying
Learning Facebook Application Development

About Packt Publishing

Packt, pronounced 'packed', published its first book "*Mastering phpMyAdmin for Effective MySQL Management*" in April 2004 and subsequently continued to specialize in publishing highly focused books on specific technologies and solutions.

Our books and publications share the experiences of your fellow IT professionals in adapting and customizing today's systems, applications, and frameworks. Our solution based books give you the knowledge and power to customize the software and technologies you're using to get the job done. Packt books are more specific and less general than the IT books you have seen in the past. Our unique business model allows us to bring you more focused information, giving you more of what you need to know, and less of what you don't.

Packt is a modern, yet unique publishing company, which focuses on producing quality, cutting-edge books for communities of developers, administrators, and newbies alike. For more information, please visit our website: www.packtpub.com.

Writing for Packt

We welcome all inquiries from people who are interested in authoring. Book proposals should be sent to authors@packtpub.com. If your book idea is still at an early stage and you would like to discuss it first before writing a formal book proposal, contact us; one of our commissioning editors will get in touch with you.

We're not just looking for published authors; if you have strong technical skills but no writing experience, our experienced editors can help you develop a writing career, or simply get some additional reward for your expertise.

Learning jQuery

ISBN: 978-1-847192-50-9   Paperback: 380 pages

jQuery: Better Interaction Design and Web
Development with Simple JavaScript Techniques

1. Create better, cross-platform JavaScript code

2. Detailed solutions to specific client-side
    problems

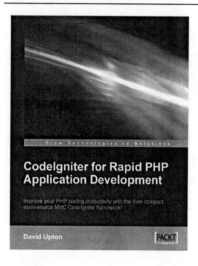

CodeIgniter for Rapid PHP
Application Development

ISBN: 978-1-847191-74-8   Paperback: 220 pages

Improve your PHP coding productivity with the free
compact open-source MVC CodeIgniter framework!

1. Clear, structured tutorial on working with
    CodeIgniter

2. Careful explanation of the basic concepts of
    CodeIgniter and its MVC architecture

3. Using CodeIgniter with databases, HTML
    forms, files, images, sessions, and email

4. Building a dynamic website quickly and easily
    using CodeIgniter's prepared code

Please check **www.PacktPub.com** for information on our titles

PHP Web 2.0 Mashup Projects

ISBN: 978-1-847190-88-8   Paperback: 280 pages

Create practical mashups in PHP grabbing and mixing data from Google Maps, Flickr, Amazon, YouTube, MSN Search, Yahoo!, Last.fm, and 411Sync.com

1. Expand your website and applications using mashups

2. Gain a thorough understanding of mashup fundamentals

3. Clear, detailed walk-through of the key PHP mashup building technologies

4. Five fully implemented example mashups with full code

Microsoft AJAX Library Essentials

ISBN: 978-1-847190-98-7   Paperback: 300 pages

A practical tutorial to enhancing the user experience of your ASP.NET web applications with the final release of the Microsoft AJAX Library

1. A rapid and practical guide to including AJAX features in your .NET applications

2. Learn practical development strategies and techniques

3. Go through a case study that demonstrates the theory you learned throughout the book

Lightning Source UK Ltd.
Milton Keynes UK
18 January 2010

148759UK00002B/44/P